Entertaining Spirits Unaware

Unaware

The End-Time Occult Invasion

"*Entertaining Spirits Unaware* will provide readers with the tools needed to effectively combat the encroachment of the occult and New Age into our lives and homes.*"*
Marlin Maddoux, host "Point of View" radio talk show

"If ever there was a need for a clear exposé on the subtle deceptions of the Evil One, it is now! This book will provide you with just such a tool. It will not gather dust in the possession of those who care.*"*
Ed Decker, author *The God Makers*

"I always appreciate Eric Barger's godly insight into the tough issues surrounding false doctrine. This book on the occult invasion is timely and much needed in our culture.*"*
**Jim Spencer, author, *Hard Case Witnessing:*
*Winning "Impossibles" for Christ***

"David and Eric's years of experience in researching and ministering on the occult and related topics will make this book a valuable resource for every household.*"*
Phil Phillips, author *Turmoil in the Toybox*

Acknowledgments

First and foremost, we thank the Lord by His Holy Spirit for insight and wisdom, giving us the vision and words for this book.

Next, we are grateful to our wonderful wives, Debbie and Melanie, and our families for patiently standing by us.

From Eric . . .

First, I want to gratefully acknowledge Wayne and Louise Ivey, for without them this book would not have become a reality.

I want to give special thanks to Ed Decker of "Saints Alive in Jesus" and Jim Spencer of "Through the Maze Ministries" for their wisdom, friendship, and insight. I also want to make a special dedication of my work in this book to the memory of Dr. Walter Martin, who taught me to be ready to give every man an answer (1 Peter 3:15).

From the bottom of my heart, I want to thank all of those who gave resources, research, inspiration, and time in prayer. Al & Myrtle Bender, Sandy Besemann, Sherri Cupples, Pastor Phil Daniels (and his "two-edged sword"!), Ty & Cheryl Davenport, Joe & Barb Fink, Don Forland, Dave Gale, Pastor Brad Howard and the faithful at Lakeshore Community Church, Pastor Milton Hubbard and everyone at Living Word, Dr. Paul & Sherri Liechty, Dr. Jim & Kay Lynn Manker, Steve & Joanne Millhorn, Margaret Moberly ("the intercessor"), Verda Rommel, James & Rhonda Samudio, Barry Schueler, Larry & Pam Semans, and so many more.

From David . . .

I would like to dedicate my portion of this book to four men who have greatly influenced me.

Dr. Jerry Falwell—The man who obeyed God in building a school, Liberty University, that produces champions. He taught me as a young Christian to never give up.

Dr. Elmer Towns—The man who has inspired me to live a holy life.

Dr. Noah Hutchings—The man who has been like a spiritual father to me. He has shared a wealth of knowledge with me. Without his friendship, this book would not be in your hands.

Dr. Terry Smith—My pastor, a man who feeds me when I am at home, and the shepherd of my family while I'm away.

Table of Contents

Introduction

Our goal in writing Entertaining Spirits Unaware: The End-Time Occult Invasion is to offer a resource concerning the occult, in particular concerning the many ways our culture is being affected by its workings. Though sometimes subtly, occultism such as witchcraft (Wicca) and the New Age movement are undoubtedly infiltrating and often capturing the masses today.

Throughout recorded history, Satan has consistently enticed mankind into his dark, supernatural realm. Aided by man's sin-driven quest for control, power, and self–enlightenment, Lucifer's lure has been quite successful. From the pages of the Old Testament, we are made aware of his many traps and catch a glimpse of individuals and entire nations caught up in his web. From Pharaoh's court to Elijah's triumph over the false prophets of Baal, the occult is pictured as the ultimate defiance of God's supremacy. From the New Testament, we see God's powerful and complete antidote, as captives are set free through the diligence of the saints in the mighty name of Jesus.

The Middle Ages saw throngs lost in the control of sorcery. For centuries, entire regions of the known world were found beholden to every fearful bondage from simple superstition to overt and hideous satanic-like rituals such as those the Druids performed. The threat of occult-based reprisals at the hands of the magicians in those days elevated Satan's cause dramatically.

Now, though claiming to have progressed to new heights, man has come full circle in the hour in which we live. Occult beliefs seem to be exploding around us and the alleged "knowledge" of the modern-day occultist is once again sought, perhaps as never before. In a time when psychic hotlines, astrology, and witchcraft seem to be the norm, and when our children find their entertainment inundated with occult practices, extreme violence, and heroes such as the fictional boy-wizard Harry Potter, Bible-believers are sure to recognize that we are indeed living in the last days. Following Peter's admonition to be "sober and vigilant" (1 Peter 5:8) is surely an important and apropos warning to us, for certainly our enemy is prowling about seeking whom he may devour before his time is gone.

We contend that the Christian, armed with God's Word and cognizant of the times in which we live, will not be overcome and can make a difference for the Kingdom of God. Based on an examination of Deuteronomy chapter eighteen, we believe that understanding the "nine forbidden practices" mentioned there is mandatory for successful Christian living in this and every era. Also, our chapters discussing other pertinent and controversial issues such as the affinity that Hollywood, television, and cartoons hold for the occult, as well as the yearly celebration of the pagan holiday Halloween, will give readers ammunition for the battles being waged for our communities, our churches, and our homes.

The Spirit of Apathy . . .

Occasionally we'll get an e-mail or comment critical of our concerns about the occult. This is to be expected from those outside Christ, but often it is directed from someone within the church. Recently, after addressing occultism in his Internet newsletter, Eric received an e-mail that said, "Why worry about Harry Potter? You should be more concerned about Austin Powers and the Back Street Boys."

Now don't misunderstand us, we *are* concerned about the fleshly effects of Hollywood and the music industry. Both of our ministries have consistently spoken out about these issues for years. But the occult is actually the very crux of the rebellion that the vast majority of today's entertainment world is peddling. This book will further demonstrate our desire to expose the ungodly nature of today's entertainment industry as we deal with coinciding issues in these pages.

We also recognize that the Enemy would love to sidetrack not only us but also the church in general. He often uses well-meaning people to accomplish this purpose, focusing only on effect instead of cause. The fact is that the occult represents the epitome of Satan's deception and manipulation over the lives of humankind. Thus it must be recognized and exposed for what it is, wherever and whenever it surfaces around us, even if it means exposing today's man-made icons which the world has accepted hook, line, and sinker.

To illustrate the contemptuous nature of the occult, one only needs to examine the Ten Commandments in Exodus, chapter twenty. The occult is literally the antithesis of God's most sacred directives to mankind, starting with the first, "Thou shalt have no other gods before me" (Exodus 20:3).

All sin flows from the act of rebellion, yet there are many Christians who sit in church year after year never understanding that the basis of *all* sin—rebellion—is biblically associated with occultism. The Bible clearly denotes that rebellion is as the sin of witchcraft (1 Samuel 15:23) and that trusting other belief systems dictates that one rebelliously follow and serve other gods. This is true whether the rebellion surfaces as Satanism, sorcery, witchcraft, or any of the variations of its end-time spin-off, the New Age movement. While the occult may have many different facets and may seem mysterious and foreign to most, the spirit behind it is nothing more than rebellion. When we realize this, Satan's veil of darkness and threat of the unknown can be seen for what it is—a shallow masquerade feebly attempting to defy Almighty God.

We'd Rather Not Either, But . . .

Granted, the occult is not a pretty subject, nor one we relish to continue ministering about. But, in a day when "itching ears" seem only to hear what pleases them, and when theological standards bend to accept every belief system as a "path to enlightenment," we recognize why the Lord has called some in His ministry to wake the sleeping church and the masses at large about the issues we raise here.

There are times when both of these authors wish that the Lord would allow us to do something "nicer," but this is the ministry He has called us both to carry out—separately in our public ministry and together in this book. And while we may daydream about presenting seminars on the grace of God or the "Sermon on the Mount," it seems that the Lord has other plans for us. Surely this is why we both feel so adamantly about these tough and confrontational issues, for were it not for the calling, guidance, and stamina of the Holy Spirit, our perseverance would have run out long ago.

So with that, we reiterate that every Christian needs to know about and have a working knowledge of the New Age, witchcraft, and the occult in our culture today. In our midst, there are captives in bondage by the millions, and as God's servants, we are *all* called to go and set them free—beginning with our own homes.

Entertaining Spirits Unaware: The End-Time Occult Invasion will first shed light on what God's Word says about these dark practices and beliefs. Then, armed with that insight, we pray you'll actively use the information and detail offered concerning some of the specifics that challenge the Christian worldview in our society today. Above all, it is our heart's cry that this book will light the path toward man's only hope and touch lives for the Kingdom of God.

—Eric Barger & David Benoit, September 2000

Part One

The Nine Forbidden Practices

Chapter 1

Nine Forbidden Practices

When thou art come into the land which the Lᴏʀᴅ thy God giveth thee, thou shalt not learn to do after the abominations of those nations. There shall not be found among you any one that maketh his son or his daughter to pass through the fire, or that useth divination, or an observer of times, or an enchanter, or a witch, Or a charmer, or a consulter with familiar spirits, or a wizard, or a necromancer. For all that do these things are an abomination unto the Lᴏʀᴅ: and because of these abominations the Lᴏʀᴅ thy God doth drive them out from before thee. Thou shalt be perfect with the Lᴏʀᴅ thy God.

—Deuteronomy 18:9–13

In the passage above, you will find the "nine forbidden practices" that the occult world utilizes. We'll be looking at each of these and will also see how these practices are being implemented all around us today. God's disdain for something is always information given for our own good. Knowing what God has warned us about will help you avoid Satan's traps and pitfalls, and we hope it will also encourage you to boldly share these truths with others. A careful study of these nine practices will give you and those of your household information needed to live more effectively for Christ, both in personal lifestyle and in advocacy in the world. Understanding these things should spur us on to be the evangelists God has called us to be as well.

Many of those lost in the occult world attempt to justify or validate the beliefs and practices they have chosen based on the simple assumption that such practices work. The thought of possibly attaining a positive outcome, such as personal power, is all that many people need to test the mystical waters of New Age occultism. When it is pointed out that the Bible vehemently warns and expressly forbids people from dabbling in the occult, some standard rebuttals are that the Bible is outdated or that the Judeo-Christian God is just a heartless, unfeeling cosmic killjoy. Others will defend the occult practices they participate in by remarking that "it isn't Satan worship," or "I don't hurt anybody." For millions who have driven down the New Age highway and exited onto "Astrology Road," "Psychic Street," or "Divination Drive," their biggest enemies are (1) a quest for unbridled power, (2) a life missing any true moral compass, and (3) ignorance of where the road really leads.

As we enter the new millennium, it is vital that we Christians have a basic understanding of what these folks have bought into. In a world steeped in moral relativism, which teaches that the only absolute is that there are *no* absolutes, the truth is often wildly unpopular. Our society has turned classic reasoning upside down in many ways. It rewards those who accept no singular religious view, but applauds the equal acceptance of every theology and religion as "tolerant." Holding to a singular view, especially historic Christian positions such as the inerrancy of the Bible and the faith-based salvation it teaches, is akin to preaching hate today. The authentic Christian's staunch and unswerving insistence that there is but one true God will either be a breath of fresh air or like fingernails grinding on a chalkboard. Yet, what are we to do? Jesus *is* Savior; His Word *is* truth; and there is but *one way* to be saved. We must accurately present the truth in word and in deed, and with the numbers of New Agers and occultists estimated to be over one hundred million today, we're sure to encounter strong opposition to our insistence of their errors. The only answer is to be prepared with answers. In a world not only inundated with each and every one of the forbidden practices outlined in Deuteronomy 18, but now *endorsing them*, it is unmistakable that we are very close to the imminent return of our Savior Jesus Christ as well. It is time for every Christian to stop waffling and choose which side we really stand on today! When it comes to the occult, ignorance isn't bliss and silence isn't golden!

One thing is certain, if we are to be faithful to our God and to the title of "Christian," we are obligated to extend the words of truth to every witch, Satanist, New Ager, and spiritual seeker, so at least they are given a fighting chance to be brought into the wonderful light of the Savior, Jesus Christ. Otherwise, they are destined to an eternity in hell. Just as the Ten Commandments are not the "Ten Suggestions," the "Great Commission" of Matthew 28:19–20 is not just an idea for us to ponder. It is a lifelong job for us to carry out.

Answers

So, is the Bible indeed "old-fashioned" and outdated? Is Jehovah a spoilsport? And is casual astrology or even nature worship akin to Satan worship? It is important to point out to anyone believing any of these things that the Mosaic books of the Bible (Genesis, Exodus, Leviticus, Numbers, and Deuteronomy) speak directly to the occult. These biblical books are perhaps the oldest religious writings on the planet. They, along with the other sixty-one books or letters that comprise the Holy Bible, are also without question the best-kept religious documents in history. The weight they carry because of the mere age of the revelation within them casts any Medieval occult literature into a dubious light at best. Though some psychics and astrologers attempt to lure unknowing prospective clients by insisting that divination and astrology are taught about in the Bible (they are, but in a totally negative light) the opposite is usually the norm. Most occult enthusiasts point out that what they believe and what they do does actually work, is cool, is the "in" thing to do, and that the Bible is outdated and far too constrictive. It is important to ask them if they realize that the Bible spoke directly to the issue of the occult well over five thousand years ago. It is also important to note that the Bible actually introduced mankind to Lucifer/Satan/the Devil. Early in Scripture, God drew a line in the sand and warned man not to cross into Satan's occult territory. He did so not as a cruel controller, but as a loving Father who wanted the very best for His children and to keep them from practices destined to bring death and destruction. Along these same lines, it is totally inconsistent for a Satanist to deny the authenticity of the Bible. To do so totally invalidates the being he claims to worship.

Though the large percentage of those who operate in the occult kingdom have been cleverly brought to believe that there is no Devil and what they practice is not satanic in nature, the fact remains that God, in His Word, clearly denounces each and every major New Age and occult practice in the world today. And if indeed the Bible is *the* truth, God verifies His warnings about the occult again and again through the words of his chosen servants. This culminates with Jesus Christ and the apostles identifying Satan as the enemy of our souls, the father of lies, and as a creature resembling a savage lion seeking whom he may devour. So, is astrology Satan worship? Not in the classic definition, but who gets the glory in the end? The Devil himself. So is there any difference? No. The tragic end result is the same. Eternal judgment and separation from God.

> Blessed are they that do his commandments, that they may have right to the tree of life, and may enter in through the gates into the city. For without [outside of Heaven] are dogs, and sorcerers [those trusting in and practicing magical arts], and whoremongers, and murderers, and idolaters [those who follow and serve other "gods"], and whosoever loveth and maketh a lie. I Jesus have sent mine angel to testify unto you these things in the churches.
>
> —Revelation 22:14–16a

Chapter 2

Forbidden Practice #1— Human Sacrifice, Abortion and the Occult

The first forbidden practice found in our keystone passage of Deuteronomy 18 is human sacrifice—"passing through the fire."

The practice of human sacrifice has been the subject of stories handed down through many cultures worldwide for centuries. Though today we only hear of occasional cases where human life is taken in religious rituals, the practice does go on. And though witches and Satanists both deny its existence in their creeds, history paints another picture.

Recently the wire services carried an article entitled "Sacrifice Victim Remains on Display." The victim spoken of in the article was over five hundred years old. The sacrificial remains of a female came from the Inca civilization in Peru. History records that the Incas did not pray to the Devil, as they were not worshippers of any deity. Instead, they worshipped nature. To appease the gods of the sun, moon, water, and earth, they would perform human sacrifices. According to the Public Broadcasting System program "Nova" (aired November 24, 1998), it is believed that the girl, frozen high in the Andes mountains, was sacrificed to the "mountain" gods. Cable TV's A&E Network has also produced a video entitled "Death Cult of the Incas." And though the Incas are regarded as one of history's most advanced cultures, it is evident that they were barbaric toward their young—all for the gratification of demon gods. So much for the standard argument witches present that those who worship nature do not sacrifice human life during rituals.

History is replete with instance after instance of human life being offered to the "god" of a tribe or people in return for protection or spiritual favor. In Old Testament times, one of the false gods widely worshipped by the pagan tribes was Molech, who was represented by a bull. In each of the eight mentions the Bible makes of this demon god, the same theme reoccurs—the death of children.

The statue of Molech that the pagan people and backslidden Israelites used as an altar had its arms extended to receive its victims. A fire would be built under the bull, which turned the arms red-hot. As the idol heated, drums would be played and the people would writhe, scream, and work themselves into a frenzy. Then at the appropriate time they would bring the selected children and hand them over to the priests of Molech. The priests would take these children and lay them on the altar, where they would burn to death. That is what is meant by "passing your children through the fire"—human sacrifice.

In December 1997 the nation of Trinidad was rocked by the gruesome discovery of graves containing human remains sacrificed in a bizarre occult ritual. Four children (and the sister of one of the murderers) were brutally killed *by their parents* in an attempt to gain riches from their demonic god.

In early 1994 we watched as TV cameras recorded the

grisly discovery of over a dozen satanic sacrifice victims, which were unearthed along the Texas-Mexico border. The killings were carried out by a drug-dealing cult who believed that the human sacrifices would give them magical protection from rival drug lords and the authorities. Considering these and numerous other examples from right here in the United States, one can imagine that death cults built around such practices as Santeria, voodoo and self-styled Satanism could be operating nearly anywhere today.

There are other instances of modern-day human sacrifice which could be cited. For example, it is well known that in some parts of India's Hindu culture, human sacrifice—especially of ex-Hindus who convert to Christianity—goes on to this day. The Kondh tribe's history of sacrifice to the Earth Goddess, in particular the killing of infant females, is well documented.

It is obvious that if we think that the "civilized world" is rid of such horrors, we need to think again. The spirit of Molech is alive and well in America today. Satan's desire to kill, steal, and destroy (John 10:10) is vividly displayed through both the emotional and physical acts of child abuse and the ultimate practice inspired by this horrific god—abortion. Abortions may not be carried out in consideration of an actual deity, but they are surely an act of human sacrifice, taking life on the altar of convenience to appease the god of "self."

Abortion is a topic laden with ancient demonic history. It is one of Satan's most intense battlefields. And if you are under the conception that all Christians view abortion and so-called women's rights the same way, you had better reconsider. The encroachment of liberalism and the endorsement of confused thinking have nearly stripped us of the inevitable fact that abortion is indeed murder.

The legislators and courts may not be able to decide when life begins, but we can assure you that the Devil knows when life begins. Few, if any, would view abortion as "child sacrifice," but indeed, the majority of abortions performed today are the end result of lifestyles given over to sin. It is a sacrifice at the hands of other "gods." The gods of "pleasure" and "convenience" are appeased with the death of human lives each day, just as Molech was satisfied millennia ago. It is the same spirit with identical results. The only difference now is that doctors—whose mission should be to save life—have become the high priests of death. Their "rituals" are performed in a hospital instead of on a "high place" described in the Bible, and the death sentence is carried out with medical instruments instead of the arms of a flaming idol.

So why would there ever be any confusion about what abortion really is in the minds of any person who claims to be a Christian? History has repeated itself again. A people, once dedicated to follow the Lord, have slipped into the trap of relativism masked by the title of "political correctness" today. Stepping over the edge to be accepted by the world and to shake the unfavorable title of "radical" or "fundamentalist," there are entire denominations today whose leadership has failed to make the truth abundantly clear to the world and who have even accepted the demonic practice of abortion as a viable "choice." Listen as the prophet Jeremiah describes Israel centuries ago, for he is surely talking about some in the church in our hour as well.

> Because of all the evil of the children of Israel and of the children of Judah, which they have done to provoke me to anger, they, their kings, their princes, their priests, and their prophets, and the men of Judah, and the inhabitants of Jerusalem. And they have turned unto me the back, and not the face: though I taught them, rising up early and teaching them, yet they have not hearkened to receive instruction. But they set their abominations in the house, which is

called by my name, to defile it. And they built the high places of Baal, which are in the valley of the son of Hinnom, to cause their sons and their daughters to pass through the fire unto Molech; which I commanded them not, neither came it into my mind, that they should do this abomination, to cause Judah to sin.

—Jeremiah 32:32–35

It is because of this grievous error—part of the great "falling away" or apostasy described in 2 Thessalonians chapter two—that God is bringing his judgment on liberalism in the church. Those who profess the name "Christian" yet accept, follow, and even participate in the world's practices, are destined to be dealt with by God, perhaps at the hands of Antichrist.

And now therefore thus saith the LORD, the God of Israel, concerning this city, whereof ye say, It shall be delivered into the hand of the king of Babylon by the sword, and by the famine, and by the pestilence.

—Jeremiah 32:36

But in God's mercy and justice, He has promised to unite those who will serve Him—the "remnant"—rewarding them and bestowing on them the title of "kings and priests" forever!

Behold, I will gather them out of all countries, whither I have driven them in mine anger, and in my fury, and in great wrath; and I will bring them again unto this place, and I will cause them to dwell safely: And they shall be my people, and I will be their God: And I will give them one heart, and one way, that they may fear me for ever, for the good of them, and of their children after them: And I will make an everlasting covenant with them, that I will not turn away from them, to do them good; but I will put my fear in their hearts, that they shall not depart from me.

—Jeremiah 32:37–40

Make no mistake; God does not think lightly about the issue of abortion. There is no mistake of the mention of Molech in this awesome and powerful passage from Jeremiah.

We are painfully aware that there will be some who read this book, who have been a participant in some way in the act of abortion. We're well aware of how volatile and emotional this issue is today and how it polarizes people into two camps. However, we also believe that if we avoid or sidestep the issue in any way, we wouldn't be true to the leading of the Lord and to pointing out the importance of recognizing abortion as it relates to Spiritual Warfare. If there is anything we need today, it is no nonsense, straightforward leadership on issues like this.

Let us also be quick to say that God is not only the God of justice, but He is also the God of mercy. By our strong stand on abortion, it should in no way be taken that these authors cut short the grace and mercy of God for those who have had abortions or in some other way have participated in them. The dividing line between wrongful death and its continuing repercussions is the wonderful blood of the Savior. Alleluia! Though the consequences of any sin may continue in the natural world, they are blunted for eternity the very moment anyone repents and comes to the cross of Christ. So, if our standard on abortion seems cold or unfeeling somehow, remember there is forgiveness and healing for all who approach the Lord and but ask.

Chapter 3

Forbidden Practice #2—
Divination (Fortune Telling)

Blessed is the man that walketh not in the counsel of the
ungodly, nor standeth in the way of sinners, nor sitteth in
the seat of the scornful. But his delight is in the law of the
Lord; and in his law doth he meditate day and night. And
he shall be like a tree planted by the rivers of water, that
bringeth forth his fruit in his season; his leaf also shall not
wither; and whatsoever he doeth shall prosper. The ungodly are not so: but are like the chaff which the wind driveth
away. Therefore the ungodly shall not stand in the judgment, nor sinners in the congregation of the righteous.

—Psalm 1:1–5

In Deuteronomy 18:10–12, Psalm 1:1, and many other passages, the Lord makes it clear that we Christians are to take
no stock in what is spoken or performed by witches, sooth-
sayers, or occultists. God makes it clear that the repercussions are great for delving into the world of divination. In
another Old Testament story, we see King Saul reduced to a
mere shadow of his former self, hopeless, faithless, and re-

sorting to fortune telling (1 Samuel 28:7–20). Perhaps this is why most people first walk into Satan's camp. They are faithless and without a true barometer of what is right and what is wrong and with no understanding of what they are really getting into—they are seeking answers for their lives.

In 1 Kings 18, we find one of the greatest accounts of God's power and disdain for witchcraft and demonic prophecy. Here, God's prophet, Elijah, challenges the wicked, yet weak King Ahab and four hundred fifty prophets of the demon god Baal to match the awesome power of Jehovah God. In this encounter we see a microcosm of what God's people have faced throughout time when confronting the powers of darkness. Let's look at this faith-building story and notice the similarities of how the world around us reacts when we point out their hell-bound lifestyle and expose the modern purveyors of the New Age and occult for what they are.

In verse seventeen, Ahab accuses Elijah of being the problem. Being denigrated for holding up a standard, Elijah was blamed for being the problem. The exact converse was true. Just as many of us who understand the necessity to "defend the faith" (Jude 3) and "expose the fruitless deeds of darkness" (Ephesians 5:11), Elijah was seen as the actual problem instead of one who held the solution. A world in conflict, lost in sin, does not often want to hear the truth about the lifestyles that they lead. Nonetheless, it is a command by the Lord to be "salt and light" during this life. Often this "salt" gets in the open wounds that a life of sin has brought to others and the reaction is much like the one King Ahab displayed here: ". . . Ahab said unto him, Art thou he that troubleth Israel?" You can count on the fact that the coming Antichrist will use the same reasoning to lure many to his side when he goes about eliminating his earthly opposition.

Elijah answered, "I have not troubled Israel; but thou, and thy father's house, in that ye have forsaken the commandments of the LORD, and thou hast followed Baalim" (1 Kings 18:18). The fact is that God's truth is NOT the problem. But it is certainly perceived as such by those who cannot stand to hear it. (Another good reason to understand Spiritual Warfare if we expect to be effective seeing the captives set free!)

As history goes, Elijah and Ahab's troop of false prophets had a type of contest, a "challenge of the prophets," if you will. This was no small event, for the Bible notes in 1 Kings 18:19–20, that all Israel gathered to watch as two altars were built; one for Elijah and one for the prophets of Baal. Wood was placed on them and the pieces of two dismembered bulls were laid on top. Then, according to Elijah's challenge, the prophets of the Devil attempted to call down fire from their god in hopes it would consume the offering that had been prepared. Their efforts were of no avail. The Bible tells us they called to their god from morning until noon and then resorted to cutting themselves, offering a blood sacrifice to their silent, powerless god. Elijah, mocking them, suggested that perhaps their god was talking and not listening to them, sleeping, or maybe on a journey. One version of the Bible denotes Elijah suggesting that the false god Baal was busy in the bathroom! Hour after hour, the false prophets tried every trick they knew, but still their god was silent. Then finally Elijah stepped up, had barrel after barrel of water poured on his sacrifice—twelve in all—and then stood by as the God of Israel moved, as we read here in 1 Kings 18:36–39.

> And it came to pass at the time of the offering of the evening sacrifice, that Elijah the prophet came near, and said, LORD God of Abraham, Isaac, and of Israel, let it be known this day that thou art God in Israel, and that I am thy servant, and that I have done all these things at thy word. Hear me, O LORD, hear me, that this people may know that thou art the LORD God, and that thou hast turned their heart back

again. Then the fire of the LORD fell, and consumed the burnt sacrifice, and the wood, and the stones, and the dust, and licked up the water that was in the trench. And when all the people saw it, they fell on their faces: and they said, The LORD, he is the God; the LORD, he is the God.

This was God's way of showing His ultimate approval of Elijah and His ultimate anger toward occultism. Verse forty tells us that Elijah then slew the false prophets by the brook Kishon—a type or picture of what happens eternally to those who dabble in magic and sorcery today.

From this account, we also glean an important fact that is paralleled in our lives today. The people of Israel had been walking in division and confusion previous to this dramatic encounter on Mount Carmel. They had been subject to bad political and spiritual leadership and it had taken its toll on their ability to make godly decisions. They had been subjected to occult teachings and supernatural manifestations. Their judgment had grown cloudy and their spirits cold to God's Word. It was showdown day and Elijah knew it.

Sounding fed up but full of God's Spirit, Elijah proclaimed:

How long halt ye between two opinions? if the LORD be God, follow him: but if Baal, then follow him. And the people answered him not a word.

—1 Kings 18:21

The silence at that moment on Mount Carmel must have been deafening, but it did not deter Elijah. In the same way, the lack of instant approval from those around us in our society or even in our churches, must not deter us from challenging the forces of darkness in order to see captives set free. Today, the church needs to take hard, sometimes unpopular positions as we stand on the Word of God. Sadly, precious few

Christian leaders take on the occult darkness and shoddy political leadership of our day. Whenever we are offered compromise in place of righteousness, our choice should be crystal clear. It is usually unpopular, and certainly not politically correct, but the world needs to know just what we stand for and also what we stand *against*. The Devil may try to stir up strife and trouble in every quadrant, but as Elijah said, "If the Lord be God, follow Him"!

How Do They Do It?

How do psychics do what they do? It is either one of two ways: they are either faking it (that is using luck or cheating at their trade) or they are indeed in touch with the spirit world. Regardless of their claims, psychics cannot actually foretell the future. Besides, when you consider it logically, even if you were psychic and actually knew the future, why would you be working for a psychic hotline, let alone in a strip mall along the highway somewhere? Wouldn't it be less trouble and more profitable to just go play the lottery?

On a television advertisement for a psychic hotline, one male customer actually blurted in amazement, "I called my psychic, and she told me my name, and where I lived, and how old I was." This wouldn't be hard to do if the psychic was privy to a computer database and telephone caller ID. Plus, if this guy doesn't know his name, where he lives, or how old he is, he doesn't need a psychic; he needs a psychiatrist! Regardless, they *say* they can foretell the future. Even their advertising says so. One series of billboard ads read, "Psychic. No appointment necessary." We presume they know when their next client is coming.

History is replete with figures who were involved with the occult. Adolph Hitler was a man well-versed in occultism and demonism. On page seventeen of the book *Gods and Beasts: The Nazis and the Occult*, we read:

The city was deluged with mediums, necromancers, and astrologers who claimed to be occupied with futuristic science which the scientific establishment was as yet unable to appreciate, since experiments were still unverified.

Edgar Cayce was a very popular psychic a few decades ago. He was known as the "Sleeping Prophet." Mr. Cayce could supposedly manipulate dreams and foretell the future through those dreams. Today, many years after his death, his teachings continue to effect many.

Concerning dreams, there were men in the Bible who both dreamed and interpreted dreams—a very popular occult practice. Daniel interpreted Nebuchadnezzar's dream in Daniel chapter four. But the difference between Daniel and psychics today is that Daniel didn't have to have any prior information to answer Nebuchadnezzar's questions concerning his dreams, and most importantly he was moved by the Spirit of God—not demons.

In Deuteronomy 13:1–3 we read:

> If there arise among you a prophet, or a dreamer of dreams, and giveth thee a sign or a wonder, And the sign or the wonder come to pass, whereof he spake unto thee, saying, Let us go after other gods, which thou hast not known, and let us serve them; Thou shalt not hearken unto the words of that prophet, or that dreamer of dreams: for the LORD your God proveth you, to know whether ye love the LORD your God with all your heart and with all your soul.

The actress Demi Moore recently wrote the foreword to her psychic's new book. Many celebrities employ personal psychics, but they are not alone. U.S. government agencies and police departments worldwide secretly use psychics. Our government allegedly spends millions each year on psychics who are supposed to be able to tell the future.

Princess Diana had her own psychic. It was tragically interesting that on the night of the automobile accident that took her life, a television news reporter commented, "Isn't that amazing? Just a couple of weeks ago she went to see her psychic." No, it's just proof that no one knows the future—no one except God.

Most people, even those who attain positions of high prestige such as Princess Diana, don't adequately understand or even know about the demonic forces that are at work to deceive them. We're in no way trying to reflect ill about Diana personally or about anyone else who used psychics. What we are saying is that she followed psychics, and these psychics were supposed to guide her life and give her happiness and fulfillment, but they could not because they do not know the future.

In Acts chapter sixteen, the Scripture speaks of the forces that are actually at work in the psychic world.

> And it came to pass, as we went to prayer, a certain damsel possessed with a spirit of divination met us, which brought her masters much gain by soothsaying: The same followed Paul and us, and cried, saying, These men are the servants of the most high God, which show unto us the way of salvation. And this did she many days. But Paul, being grieved, turned and said to the spirit, I command thee in the name of Jesus Christ to come out of her. And he came out the same hour.
>
> —Acts 16:16–18

As we pointed out, authentic psychics are empowered by demonic spirits who feed them information with a dual goal in mind—to deceive the hearer and to tempt them into a life dependent on the occult instead of God.

It is interesting that Paul and Silas were beaten and imprisoned for casting the demon out of the girl in Acts 16. We believe that in the times ahead of us, we'll see this same sort of activity take place once again. We believe it will someday be considered bigoted and illegal to cast demons out of people. This is nearly where America is today, and sadly, many in the church give unbelieving disapproval to any ministry who takes seriously the challenge of "setting the captives free."

> And when her masters saw that the hope of their gains was gone, they caught Paul and Silas, and drew them into the marketplace unto the rulers, And brought them to the magistrates, saying, These men, being Jews, do exceedingly trouble our city, And teach customs, which are not lawful for us to receive, neither to observe, being Romans. And the multitude rose up together against them: and the magistrates rent off their clothes, and commanded to beat them. And when they had laid many stripes upon them, they cast them into prison, charging the jailor to keep them safely: Who, having received such a charge, thrust them into the inner prison, and made their feet fast in the stocks.
>
> —Acts 16:19–24

Divination is not a gift. The psychic hotlines all claim to have the most gifted psychics. In reality, they do not have gifted psychics; they have people who are either demon possessed or charlatans. The girl spoken of in Acts 16 was possessed by the spirit of divination. You'll notice that she was acting as if she was a very religious person, saying, "These men are of God." Some may wonder what was wrong with that. Even though she *was* speaking the truth, Paul recognized that it really wasn't her speaking at all. It was a force from hell who had taken over her body and was channeling through her. Paul didn't want the works of God or his preaching to be associated with demonism. He commanded the demon to come out of her, never speaking to the woman directly, but addressing only the spirit that had bound her.

Now the question remains: During the time when this girl was possessed by the demonic spirit, could she actually know the future? Again the answer is no, but by using the girl's body and voice the invading demon could attempt to manipulate the future. We need to be crystal clear on this—demons attempt to *manipulate* the future; they cannot *foretell* the future.

So, the next time you see an ad on TV, a billboard advertisement for a psychic hotline, or happen by a booth at your local county fair offering fortune telling, tarot card reading, or other psychic sensations, remember—whether it's by demons or through trickery—those attempting to remove money from your pocket in return for foreknowledge *do not* know the future. Instead, the Bible foretells theirs.

> He that overcometh shall inherit all things; and I will be his God, and he shall be my son. But the fearful, and unbelieving, and the abominable, and murderers, and whoremongers, and **sorcerers**, and idolaters, and all liars, shall have their part in the lake which burneth with fire and brimstone: which is the second death.
>
> —Revelation 21:7–8

Chapter 4

Forbidden Practice #3— Astrology

And lest thou lift up thine eyes unto heaven, and when thou seest the sun, and the moon, and the stars, even all the host of heaven, shouldest be driven to worship them, and serve them, which the LORD thy God hath divided unto all nations under the whole heaven.

—Deuteronomy 4:19

The third forbidden practice found in Deuteronomy 18 is "observer of times"—astrology.

In much of the ancient pagan world, astrology and the accompanying myths and superstitions were a part of daily life. The Bible records that upon seeing the crippled man healed in Acts 14, the Lystrian crowd began wildly declaring that Paul and Barnabas were "gods" named "Mercurius" and "Jupiter." This is just one example where we see occult mysticism apparently present in an entire culture. If you haven't noticed, astrology has become very popular and commonly accepted in America. According to a recent Gallup poll, thirty–two million Americans trust in astrology, about one of every five Americans. There are presently three times as many astrologers as there are clergymen in the Roman Catholic Church. Over ten thousand people work as astrologers full-time, and another two hundred thousand work as part-time astrologers. Three out of every four newspapers in the United States carry a daily horoscope.

History records a different picture than that which either Chinese or Western astrologers would like to admit. The earliest references to the mythological significance of the Greek constellations may be found in the works of Homer, which probably date to the seventh century B.C. In *The Iliad*, for instance, Homer describes the creation of Achilleus's shield by the craftsman god Hephaistos:

> On it he made the earth, and sky, and sea, the weariless sun and the moon waxing full, and all the constellations that crown the heavens, Pleiades and Hyades, the mighty Orion and the Bear, which men also call by the name of Wain: she wheels round in the same place and watches for Orion, and is the only one not to bathe in Ocean.
>
> —*Iliad XVIII*, 486–490

However, by the fifth century B.C., most of the constellations had come to be associated with myths, and the Catasterismi of Eratosthenes completed the mythologization of the stars. "At this stage, the fusion between astronomy and mythology is so complete, that no further distinction is made between them"—the stars were no longer merely identified with certain gods or heroes, but actually were perceived as divine (Seznec, 37–40).

It is easy to imagine the influence and impact that the stars made on ancient man. But with the technological advances and abundance of information today, one has to conclude that the occult and astrology, in particular, might be nearly as popular today as it was nearly three thousand years ago. Yet, the fact remains just how inconsistent astrologers have been in making their predictions. And no wonder—their science is atrocious!

Dutch researcher Kees Noorlander states:

> Some astrologers do not base their predictions on the stars, but more on the positions of the planets during a birthday or other special dates. However, there is no reason to expect an influence of the planets on your life. For instance, ebb and flow are caused by the moon and the sun, but not by the planets. So the planets cannot influence your life. But even in the hypothetical case that there is an influence of the planets, which of the planets are important? Formerly astrologers used the sun, the moon, Mercury, Venus, Mars, Jupiter and Saturn. But in the last centuries they discovered new planets: Uranus in 1781, Neptune in 1846 and Pluto in 1930. And the number of planets is not complete yet. The astronomers expect a tenth planet, which is too dark to see now. So astrologers, who base their predictions on the planets have many problems too.
>
> —see: *http://home.wxs.nl/~keesnoor/indexeng.htm*

On Noorlander's web site, he displays a very helpful chart showing how the different astrological signs have no correlation with the actual physical science of the stars. In some cases, a person actually claiming to be an Aries may actually be born during the astronomical period of the fish or Pisces. In their decision to bluntly ignore the scientific truth, astrologers show the depth of their deception. Granted, by doing so it would be an admittance that for hundreds of years astrologers have been following completely flawed charts and ideas, but most who operate in this occult art would rather not be confused by the facts. Sounds rather like demons at work doesn't it?

Though David did not have a Christian background growing up in Louisiana, he used to sit outside at night and look at the stars, and think, "If there is a God that could put these stars up there, He deserves my praise." On the other hand, Eric didn't give astrology much thought until he started getting involved with it in the early seventies. His mother, who had turned away from the Lord and religiously read her daily horoscope, influenced him. Soon, his life as a professional musician seemed to evolve around occult and mystic beliefs, in particular the horoscope that a bona fide witch had drawn for him on a scroll. If your child watches children's shows such as *The Lion King*, he or she may soon be just as Eric was, hooked on astrology. In one scene during the movie, the lead character, Simba, and his father are walking through the darkness after Simba had just disobeyed his father. They look up to the stars, and his father says to Simba, "Those are ascended kings who are willing to guide you." From the shelves in the children's section at your public library, to the hit movies and toys today, the occult is being endorsed and promoted to our kids. God help us to deflect this kind of New Age indoctrination away from them that they would grow up strong in the Lord instead!

What does the Bible say as a warning?

> And he built altars for all the host of heaven in the two courts of the house of the Lord. And he caused his children to pass through the fire in the valley of the son of Hinnom: also he observed times, and used enchantments, and used witchcraft, and dealt with a familiar spirit, and with wizards: he wrought much evil in the sight of the Lord, to provoke him to anger.
>
> —2 Chronicles 33:5–6

Who would do such a thing? It was the son of King Hezekiah,

the man who loved God so much, and whom God loved so much that He extended his life on planet Earth. His son, Manassas, got involved in astrology. In so doing, he also got involved in witchcraft and sorcery, and then digressed into practicing human sacrifice. Astrology doesn't just lead you to occultism—it *is* occultism. In fact, every person that adhered to astrology in the Bible always found themselves involved in deeper occult practices.

Just as in Hezekiah's case, there is no guarantee that just because you, as a parent, follow the Lord that your offspring will. But if there was ever a reason to grasp what is taught in Scripture and what we are attempting to explain in this book, it is for our kids and grandkids. As we have said to varying extents, the eternal outcome of others does depend on our willingness and obedience to commit to Spiritual Warfare. Only God knows how many evil acts are averted because we were dedicated; we prayed and then we acted accordingly as He led.

In the same perverted thinking that we touched on in the discussion of divination, some would insinuate that the reason they follow astrology is because they believe the wise men (the Magi) who brought gifts to baby Jesus followed astrology. After all, didn't they follow a star to Bethlehem to find Jesus? But how could this supernatural onetime act of God be construed as God's endorsement of the zodiac? God—Creator of the Stars—could certainly use them if He so desired, but when one examines the *whole* counsel of God through Scripture, it becomes vividly clear that God abhors His creatures following chance advice whose origin lies in the occult world.

It is dangerous to build your belief system on a single scripture taken out of context. This is how cults are born. It is just as dangerous to pick and choose which Bible verses one wants to follow and which ones can be ignored or which verses can be twisted to attempt proving one's own anti-biblical views and still claim they are following the Lord. This brings to mind the now-famous statements by New Age author and actress Shirley MacLaine from her "Connecting with Your Higher Self" seminars. Speaking to sold-out hotel ballroom audiences in the 1980s, Ms. MacLaine insisted time and again that reincarnation was originally taught in the Bible, but it had been taken out centuries ago by man. She proclaimed that in John 3:7, the great "ascended master" Jesus, actually said: "You must be born again . . . and again . . . and again . . . and again." The only problem is, the ancient texts say nothing of the sort. In fact, reincarnation is the antithesis of the resurrection. It's one or the other, but not both, and humans have no vote on the matter. Since reincarnation or its parent, Hindu transmigration, is never mentioned in the Bible, we can rest assured that we'll not be coming back in any other form, human or otherwise, for a second go at life in mortal bodies.

If you are involved in astrology, demonism, or witchcraft, let us assure you that you can put your troubles and burdens on the altar of Jesus Christ, and He will totally turn you around and lead you to a brand-new life. How wonderful to no longer call yourself an Aries or a Libra, but instead answer to the title of "Christian" instead! When you come to Jesus, you won't need the stars, because you have found the Creator of the stars.

Chapter 5

Forbidden Practice #4— An Enchanter

The fourth forbidden practice found in Deuteronomy 18 is an "enchanter"—someone who casts spells and incantations, whether to do good or evil. The next section on witchcraft will deal directly with this forbidden practice, so please read on.

Chapter 6

Forbidden Practice #5— Witchcraft

The fifth forbidden practice in Deuteronomy is witchcraft. Though all of us have heard the term before, it will be helpful to define witchcraft and some associated words. Here is how *Merriam-Webster's Collegiate Dictionary* defines "witchcraft."

Word Date: before 12th century
1) a) the use of sorcery or magic; b) communication with the devil or with a familiar
2) an irresistible influence or fascination
3) WICCA

Again, in *Merriam-Webster's* we find the word "witch" described as follows:

Word Date: before 12th century
1) one that is credited with usually malignant supernatural powers; especially: a woman practicing usually black witchcraft often with the aid of a devil or familiar: associate words—SORCERESS, WARLOCK

In today's culture, we often hear the word "Wicca" in relation with witchcraft. *Merriam-Webster* defines "Wicca" as follows:

Word Date: 1959
1) a religion influenced by pre-Christian beliefs and practices of western Europe that affirms the existence of supernatural power (as magic) and of both male and female deities who inhere in nature, and that emphasizes ritual observance of seasonal and life cycles.

From our nearly forty years of combined study on the New Age movement and the occult, we feel that New Age should be categorized here. The differences between New Age and Wicca are primarily in that New Agers often practice singularly and not in groups or covens. Though we recognize that what one person calls "New Age" the next may not, and that many witches would vehemently disagree with our inclusion of New Agers in their ranks, there are too many similarities to resist doing so. Communication with spirits for power and direction, worship of the earth and elements, utilization of occult practices, and other similarities are too obvious to ignore. Perhaps the main difference is that witches and warlocks most often view their roots in Europe, while New Agers often mirror their beliefs as taught by Eastern mystics. But when one researches witchcraft and New Age beliefs, it becomes strikingly clear that Satan's handprint is woven throughout.

It is of interest that as we compiled this research, we viewed one New Age web site on the Internet that had logged over EIGHT MILLION hits in just six months time. Anyone out there think the New Age is shrinking? No way!

Again using *Merriam-Webster's* definition, "New Age" is:

Word Date: 1956
1) of, relating to, or being a late 20th century social move-
    ment drawing on ancient concepts especially from East-
    ern and American Indian traditions and incorporating
    such themes as holism, concern for nature, spirituality,
    and metaphysics

While we were defining words related to witchcraft, we came
across an interesting term that has its roots in the ancient
craft. It is *"victim."* The *Merriam-Webster* definition for the
word is:

Word Date: 15th century
1) a living being sacrificed to a deity or in the performance
    of a religious rite

Though we certainly use the word "victim" differently today,
it is interesting to see that historically a "victim" described a
life taken through witchcraft. This sure flies contrary to what
we've heard modern witches drone over and over again. Every witch either of us have ever come in contact with claims
to be benevolent and always out for the "good" of man. But
just as Anton LaVey, founder of the American Satanic Church
and author of *The Satanic Bible* once said, "There is no such
thing as 'white' magic—*it's all black!*" This is the only statement he ever made that these authors agree with!

Doctrines of Demons
So what do witches really believe? First of all, witches today
claim not to believe in the Devil, because the Devil is a biblical personality. Instead they communicate with and *claim* to
manipulate spirits from another dimension. Sounds mysterious, ominous, and veiled, doesn't it?

Well, not all witches operate in the back room of some

occult bookstore in a seedy neighborhood. Take the pro-claimed witch and author Laurie Cabot for example. In 1977, after being consistently turned down for an official appoint-ment by the Salem, Massachusetts, City Council, Cabot side-stepped local authorities and personally convinced Gover-nor Michael Dukakis to appoint her the official "Witch of Salem." In fact, not only did Dukakis go against the local authorities and declare her the official witch of the town best known for the 1692 witch trials and subsequent executions, he gave her a commendation for public service! Talk about being under a spell! (See *http://www.forerunner.com/champi-on/X0043_ Witchcraft_and_Polit.html* for entire story.)

As the appointed "Witch of Salem," Cabot has become arguably the highest profiled pagan in America, perhaps the world. Appearing often on shows such as "60 Minutes" and a variety of magazine programs, she has brought witchcraft into the public eye and no doubt drawn many to view it with less skepticism and more acceptance. Not long ago, NBC's "Sunday Today" program featured a story which depicted Cabot actually conjuring spirits.

In the ceremony, using a pentacle as an amulet (a conduit for power), Cabot chanted: "Earth . . . air . . . fire . . . and water . . . and the Great Spirit, I invoke the god and goddess within my body." This sounds nearly identical to and certain-ly could be an apt description of what New Agers believe. During his live seminars, Eric has for years defined the New Age as "any system of belief that tells you to look *inside your-self* for enlightenment, wisdom, or power." The same could be said for witchcraft as well.

You'll notice that Cabot called on the spirits of the earth, air, fire, water, and of course goddess worship, the god and goddess within her. Goddess and earth worship, demonism, the New Age, and witchcraft may have their own distinctives, but in reality they all go hand in hand. She prayed to five spirits—the spirit of earth, wind, fire, water, and the "Great Spirit" within. This is a perfect example of paganism through the ages. The pentacle or five-pointed star pointing upward, which she used in the ritual, is the primary symbol of witchcraft. The five points of the pentacle represent earth, wind, fire, water, and spirit. Those are the five elementals of witchcraft.

Witches also believe in directional spirits. In the video *The Occult Experience*, a group of witches perform a ceremony in which they say:

> We call the spirits of north, from the home of the northern winds and spectacular lights. Bless this sacred space with your gifts of groundedness and forgiveness. . . . We call the spirits of west, land of the setting sun, of the moon and the oceans, of the waters within our minds and our bodies. Bring us intuition within this circle. . . . Spirits of south, arise in us, consecrate this temple of the earth.

Not only do they pray to the earth, wind, fire, water, and invoke the goddess spirit, but there are also four directional spirits—the spirits of the north, south, east, and west that witches beckon. Isaiah 43 seems to confirm this as well as God portrays doing battle for His people.

> For I am the LORD thy God, the Holy One of Israel, thy Saviour: I gave Egypt for thy ransom, Ethiopia and Seba for thee. Since thou wast precious in my sight, thou hast been honourable, and I have loved thee: therefore will I give men for thee, and people for thy life. Fear not: for I am with thee: I will bring thy seed from the east, and gather thee from the west; I will say to the north, Give up; and to the south, Keep not back: bring my sons from far, and my daughters from the ends of the earth. . . .
>
> —Isaiah 43:3–6

We might note that the politically powerful hyper–environmentalists have adopted many of the tenets of witchcraft as well. This movement, based around earth worship, sprang forth from the so-called "enlightenment" of the 1960s hippie era and has gained uncanny influence around us. Falling in line as part of the New Age movement, the environmentalists have managed to position themselves as a power lobby in our state houses and federal government, including the vice presidency (Al Gore).

Disregarding the weight of credible scientific study, the hyper-environmentalists have been able to pass legislation and see regulations put in place, that if left unchecked, surely threaten America's prominence and along with it our autonomy and freedom. The unwarranted overregulation on commerce and industry gravely hampers our ability to stand as the last superpower—the only roadblock between freedom and the enslavement of the New World Order.

Incredibly, by garnering the ear of the mass media and by ignoring sound science, this movement has been more than disingenuous to accomplish its goals. Let us never forget that the impetus for the environmentalists all began with its basis in New Age witchcraft. Now, following the motto of "victory at any cost"—including lying, they have become a powerhouse doing Satan's bidding and forwarding his end-time agenda.

The Promotion of a Religion and "Another" Jesus

Witches claim that their religion is older than Christianity by about twenty-five hundred years. It is not a new religion. But modern America has opened their arms wide to it today. Does anyone remember "Late Night" starring Joan Rivers that some years ago featured the initiation of a young girl into a coven of witches? It was live for America to see and was some of the best advertising the Devil could ever get. Of course, you would never hear any mention of someone being *delivered* from witchcraft. That would be questioned with frowns and curiosity, for the accepted thing is to get *into* it instead. In fact, the current attitude is fast becoming to accept witchcraft as normal and scorn Christianity as cult-like. Anything is possible when the First Lady of the United States, Hillary Clinton, and her personal medium, a Texan named Jean Houston, proceed to engage in a séance on the roof of the White House in an effort to contact deceased former First Lady Eleanor Roosevelt. What strange and troubling times we live in when the world around us thinks nothing of this and accepts these philosophies and practices that have been shunned throughout history. Perhaps events like this shouldn't surprise us as we speed toward the time of Antichrist's reign.

In a recent poll, teens were asked what supernatural phenomena they believed in. Seventy-four percent believe in angels; fifty percent believe in ESP; twenty-nine percent believe in witchcraft; and twenty-two percent believe in ghosts. This shows us that witchcraft is quickly becoming an acceptable religion among young people. It is perfectly acceptable in the public school system today for a witch to come and speak of her religion, but it is unacceptable for a Christian to come and speak in opposition.

The *United States Chaplain's Manual* has a section in it devoted entirely to witchcraft. Why? Because it is a religion. This manual gives a list of dates for Wiccan holidays: spring equinox, summer solstice, autumn equinox, winter solstice, candlemas, May eve, lamas, and Halloween.

In the popular *Flashpoint* newsletter, we found an article from the June 9, 1992, edition which stated:

> The kids at a public school in Portland, Oregon, were not allowed to celebrate a traditional Christmas this last year. School authorities decided that would be wrong. Religion is not permissible in the classroom. Church and state must

be kept separate. RIGHT? Since Christmas is a Christian holiday, school officials decided that the very word "Christmas" must be forbidden to be spoken. And in the place of the annual Christmas event, the school's kids would be required instead to participate in a Winter Solstice Program. On December 19, 1991, the Winter Solstice was celebrated in the school's auditorium. The theme: "To celebrate the return of light." The cover of the official printed program handed out to students and their parents was revealing. It depicted the Sun God (Lucifer) and the Moon Goddess (see Revelation 17—mystery Babylon). In one segment of the school's Solstice Program, kids came in with bar codes stamped on their foreheads. The bar code of some was read and accepted. But other children who did not have the proper mark were rejected. Only those who had the chosen mark were deemed "good and worthy." Inside the printed program is found this description of the Winter Solstice program: "Each child will partake of the sun and moon cake before entering the auditorium, where they will seat themselves according to their astrological signs. . . . Chanting will begin on entering the auditorium. . . . The Sun God and Moon Goddess will enter with attendants."

In our public schools today, children can't talk about Christmas openly because it has Christ in it, but they can talk all they please about witchcraft, sorcery, sun gods and moon goddesses, and the like.

Jeremiah 44 reflects the account of Jeremiah prophesying God's will in warning Judah to abandon the pagan practices of Egypt.

Then all the men which knew that their wives had burned incense unto other gods, and all the women that stood by, a great multitude, even all the people that dwelt in the land of Egypt, in Pathros, answered Jeremiah, saying, As for the word that thou hast spoken unto us in the name of the LORD, we will not hearken unto thee. But we will certainly do whatsoever thing goeth forth out of our own mouth, to burn incense unto the queen of heaven, and to pour out drink offerings unto her, as we have done, we, and our fathers, our kings, and our princes, in the cities of Judah, and in the streets of Jerusalem: for then had we plenty of victuals, and were well, and saw no evil. But since we left off to burn incense to the queen of heaven, and to pour out drink offerings unto her, we have wanted all things, and have been consumed by the sword and by the famine. And when we burned incense to the queen of heaven, and poured out drink offerings unto her, did we make her cakes to worship her, and pour out drink offerings unto her, without our men?

—Jeremiah 44:15–19

In these verses, we read of their rebellious rejection of the man of God. Notice that the people claim that as long as they burnt incense to the queen of heaven their needs were met, but when they stopped because of Jeremiah's insistence, their bounty dried up. This is a great example of how unregenerate hearts cling to their source of supply—even if they *know* it is wrong. The reason Israel's barns were barren once they stopped their goddess worship is clear. Even though they had ceased their pagan worship, their hearts were still unrepentant of so blatantly breaking God's commandment: "Thou shalt have no other gods before me" (Exodus 20:3). A change of deed is a start, but a change of heart is what God is really seeking from us all.

This is a classic example in Scripture that refers to feminism and goddess worship. The people—led by the women—went out and purposed to worship outside of God. They worshiped femininity, just like the feminist movement does today. (In fairness, we should point out that not all feminists are goddess worshipers or witches, but there is no doubt a correlation.)

Helping to forward the cause of witchcraft, the culture around us is moving into a new phase in these end-times. Those around us are becoming increasingly intolerant of Christianity. This is regardless of the fact that Christianity is much more tolerant of other religions (including witchcraft) than other religions are to Christianity. Some people—perhaps even our friends and loved ones—do *not* want to hear the truth when it comes to belief systems, sound doctrine, demons, or Satan. Regardless of the opposition, there are souls to fight for and we must remain adamant and vocal in the fight. Again, it is our job to expose the flaws that permeate witchcraft, New Age philosophy, and the cults while lifting up Jesus as the only way to be saved.

It often frustrates and angers witches, cultists, and secularists when, because by the nature of our faith, we stick to the biblical line of thought. Jesus is mentioned with much favor in New Age circles. New Agers envision Him as a great teacher, and mystics from all cultures see Him as one of them—possessing the "Christ consciousness." While Jesus is viewed as a great name in history, and while He is nearly always revered for *part* of what He taught, all the "warm fuzzies" any patronizing pagan might have about Him fade when the whole counsel of His teaching is brought to light. Once the glow wears off and those paying only lip service to the Lord see exactly what He *really* taught, they sing a very different tune. The *real* Jesus thins the audience considerably. Instead of the authentic and powerful King, who calls men to repent and casts out devils, people want only the Jesus holding a baby lamb or the one we envision in the manger at Christmas. The reaction to who He *really* is, as opposed to who some pagans *think* He was, is usually shock and disbelief. What has happened is that just as forewarned in Scripture, the New Age teaches a *different Jesus*, with a *different gospel* and the erroneous teaching is advanced by a *different spirit* (2 Corinthians 11:3–4). When a misinformed New Ager—under Satan's control—gets the whole picture, it's almost as if Jesus had actually taught in John 8:32, "Ye shall know the truth and the truth shall make you mad"!

The point is that witchcraft and paganism are advancing rapidly and are becoming increasingly more vocal in their opposition to Christianity. But did we expect a party? No. It is our obligation to present the unmitigated *truth* whether or not it's politically incorrect or offensive to the hearer. We needn't be coarse or abrasive in our presentation of the facts, but drawing the lost to the cross is the responsibility of the Holy Spirit, so we can't afford to get sidetracked from our part of the bargain, no matter how many witches call us "intolerant." Watering down the truth in an effort to find middle ground is the first step on the way to losing your bearings spiritually.

For all these years, these two authors have confidently preached the Word of God. We both believe that when the Bible is stacked against any other religious teaching and honestly studied, that God's truth will indeed shine through. However, the sheer numbers are so one-sided, it is simply amazing to us.

In one survey we made of a public library, this is what we found:

- Eighty-seven books on astrology, and not one to oppose it;
- Thirty-five books on witchcraft, and not one to oppose it;
- Seventy-nine books on dreams and interpreting dreams, and not one to oppose it;
- Thirty-four books on reincarnation, and not one to oppose it;
- Seventy-six books on the occult, with only one showing the

Christian view;
- And five books on goddess worship, and not one to oppose it.

David very politely donated a copy of his book, *Fourteen Things Witches Hope Parents Never Find Out*, to the library. However, when it was presented to the librarian, she said that it would have to go before the review board. The result was that it was rejected. David was informed that the book was not for public or school libraries, but rather for home or church libraries. We know the word censorship is bandied about much today, but what else can you call it? This is yet another clear-cut case of the promotion of witchcraft and the denial of Christianity to our culture.

Perhaps the best promotion given to the New Age/occult world view during the 1990s was the release of (then) Senator Al Gore's book, *Earth in the Balance: Ecology and the Human Spirit*. The fact that a U.S. senator would write such a book was, for pagans, on a scale with Shirley MacLaine's book and 1986 TV mini-series, *Out on a Limb*.

Two quotes from Gore's book will suffice to make the point that his claim to be a Baptist is wide of the mark by light years. We guarantee that he didn't learn what he imparted on the pages from spending time in a Baptist Sunday school!

Though Gore says many outrageous things in the book (such as his desire to see the internal combustion engine eliminated by the year 2015!), we will focus on two quotes that advance the pantheistic ideals that witches and New Agers hold dear. The first quote is found on page 262 and along with other passages in the book show Gore's promotion and acceptance of the idea that all religious systems must be included to fight the "evil" material establishment.

> The richness and diversity of our religious tradition throughout history is a spiritual resource long ignored by people of

faith, who are often afraid to open their minds to teachings first offered outside their own system of belief. But the emergence of . . . an intense new interest in the different perspectives on life in other cultures . . . has spurred a renewed investigation of the wisdom distilled by all faiths. This pan-religious perspective may prove especially important where our global civilization's responsibility to the earth is concerned.

Next, as Gore summarizes his thoughts, we find him making perhaps the most telling statement in the book on the very last page.

My own faith is rooted in an unshakable belief in God as creator and sustainer; a deeply personal interpretation of, and relationship with, Christ, and an awareness of a constant and holy spiritual presence in all people, all life and in all things.

"Spiritual presence . . . in all things"—Ladies and gentlemen, that is as clear an endorsement of pantheism as you will ever find. And pantheism is perhaps the glue that connects and holds witches, New Agers, and occultists together. Note as well that in the pantheistic world view, since I am a god and since you are a god (along with presumably every other living creature), there is then no personal creator, such as Jehovah God to be accountable to, and certainly no supreme divine revelation unless one has it himself. Thus, lifestyle and morals are relative and life can be lived however one pleases without thought of eternal judgment. Very convenient—until you breathe your last breath. With this kind of moral attitude, it is obvious that Gore was indeed a perfect match to be Bill Clinton's running mate and partner in crime for eight years.

Can a Witch Be a Christian?

For a moment, please look back again at that last quote from Gore's book. Notice he claims that his faith is rooted in God . . . okay. That God is his Creator and Sustainer . . . so far that's right, too. But to be able to write the absolutely wacky environmental and scary spiritual ideas Gore comes up with in the book, he *had* to qualify his ideas about Christianity by saying his religion was based on a "deeply personal interpretation of and relationship with Christ. . . ." Bingo. To the biblically–versed believer, red flags should now be flying wildly.

Private, not biblical, interpretations are what the cults are built on. That's how we came to know names like Joseph Smith, Charles Taze Russell, Jim Jones, and David Koresh. When we diverge from orthodox, first century Christianity, and decide to build our own religion using a few spare parts gleaned from Christianity, we have walked right into the kingdom of the cults. We can call what we have concocted "Christian" all we like, but if the "fruit inspection" finds mold and flies everywhere, it should be called what it is—New Age. Here's the bottom line: man must take God on God's terms, *not* on ours.

Naomi R. Goldenberg is a feminist theologian whose book, *Changing of the Gods*, looks at the future of religion, declaring that feminists will eventually overthrow existing patriarchal religions, placing divinity within the individual and establishing a new mysticism. Obviously, she is not forwarding the idea that a witch can become a true, born-again Christian. However, there are many pagans who try to blend their beliefs with Christianity. This kind of thinking can account for the high instances of Santeria, or Caribbean voodoo, found within the Catholic Church along the Eastern seaboard of the United States. It is a direct result of those emigrating from the islands who don't bother to check their paganism at customs, but instead bring it in the church.

In her book, Goldenberg writes about an acquaintance who has attempted a strange mix of paganism and Christianity for dubious reasons. She states:

> I have one close friend for whom the father-god is very important, even though she is a worshipper in the Sisterhood of Wicca. My friend readily admits that she still needs the father. "I can't get angry at the Goddess," she told me. "I need the Goddess to love and pray to. But I need a male god to scream at for making life so sad. I know this is a primitive way to think—to make the Goddess all good and the male god all bad, but that's how I feel."

Another famous witch, Selena Fox, of Milwaukee, Wisconsin, adamantly believes that a part of her is "still Christian." She states:

> Most of the Christians I know personally are certainly very loving, and they have Christ's message of love present. Just because I'm a Wiccan minister now doesn't mean that I have thrown Christianity out of my life. I had a born-again experience when I was nine years old. I was Southern Baptist. . . . I was very involved. I even gave a sermon when I was sixteen years old in a Southern Baptist church as part of Youth Sunday.

In an interview (which was picked up by Associated Press International), David was asked where he found the heaviest concentration of witchcraft and demonism in America to be. His answer surprised many people: The Bible Belt. But when you think about it, who is more susceptible to witchcraft—someone who has never heard the gospel, or someone who has had the spirit of religion in the form of church influence their growing up years?

Perhaps we, the church, are partially responsible for some of these kids turning to the occult. Though they are free moral agents, we hear stories every week of kids or young adults who have slipped into Satan's grasp, seemingly fresh off the Sunday school bus. Maybe the hypocrisy they've experienced has turned them away or maybe they've craved for the supernatural God of the universe to touch them in a real and tangible way, but because of the limitations man has placed on God, they've come up void. Regardless, it is evident that the church hasn't met the needs of many of our kids and, in turn, many of our adults. In the end though, it is the responsibility of each of us individually to seek after and follow God. No witches or New Agers will be able to place the blame on anyone but themselves come judgment day. We'd just like to see less of them stand before God's judgment in terror after a lifetime of occultism.

Selena Fox was one of the "church" kids we're describing. She claims she was "saved at a Southern Baptist church." But was she really saved? There are a lot of people who sit in good churches each week who never commit their lives to Jesus.

It is a dangerous thing to watch from the congregation, week after week, year after year, as others constantly surrender their lives to Christ, all the while knowing that God is talking to you, too. The reason: spiritual desensitization sets in. People pick up a form of godliness, but in the end deny the power of God to salvation (2 Timothy 3:5). Most likely, Fox went through the motions, *appearing* as if she had committed her life to Christ, but salvation isn't a set of actions, the keeping of rules, or the doing of religious rituals. It is a decision deep within the heart.

Recently a sixteen-year-old girl handed David a note at one of his meetings. This note read:

Dear Reverend:

I understand your stand on witchcraft, but I have a question for you. Have you ever put your arms around a tree and let that inanimate object's strength absorb your pain as you pray? Have you ever allowed an animal to comfort you with their thoughtless affections? As an herbalist and a very calm person, I am not going to get offensive. I would just like to say that not all of your witches are evil. I am a Christian, and yet I meditate. I study herbalism, and I do attempt to stay in touch with God's world. I could not curse you; I could not bless you. So the question is, am I a good witch or a bad witch?

She claims that she is a Christian and a witch too. In fact, many witches consider Jesus to be one of their own. Here is what Selena Fox has to say about Jesus in the video entitled *The Occult Experience:*

A few months ago a national Catholic newspaper interviewed me. The first thing I said to them was that Jesus Christ was a witch, and I talked to them about how the path of Wicca and its love consciousness is real similar to what Christ was espousing.

Is that what Jesus was espousing? When you are dealing with witchcraft and the occult, you have to use the Word of God as your criteria. The Devil is a master of philosophical ideas. He was able to deceive and persuade one-third of the angels to rebel with him, leave heaven, and seal their fate in hell. He is a very smart creature and will stop at nothing, including using the Scripture to lure you. This is exactly what he tried to do against Jesus during the temptation in the wilderness (see Matthew 4). He sometimes subtly, and other times boldly, perverts the Word of God. Regardless to what extent it is, by his perversions he destroys the truth. Occultists that believe they are Christians and that Jesus was a witch are prime examples fulfilling the warning of Isaiah 5:20–21.

> Woe unto them that call evil good, and good evil; that put darkness for light, and light for darkness; that put bitter for sweet, and sweet for bitter! Woe unto them that are wise in their own eyes, and prudent in their own sight!

To claim there is any such thing as a "Christian witch" is like saying "Christian pornography," "Christian cocaine," or "Christian adultery." They are mutually exclusive beliefs that can have no fellowship together.

First Samuel 15:23 says this: "For rebellion is as the sin of witchcraft. . . ." God's Word declares that rebellion is *equal* to witchcraft. Rebellion against God is now and has always been the underlying motivation for all witchcraft. How then can witchcraft—*any witchcraft*—be good or acceptable? According to God, it stems directly from rebellion—the first sin.

No, the truth is that witchcraft is an outgrowth of mankind wanting to maintain ultimate control. It was this same control that caused the fall of man in the Garden (Genesis 3). It was the same control that caused Lucifer—an angel of God—to rise up and lead a revolt in heaven. And it will be the same control that will account for the billions who will someday stand before the Great White Throne judgment described in Revelation 21, their awful doom ahead because they failed to surrender and come to a place of obedience to Jesus Christ.

Chapter 7

Forbidden Practice #6—
Charmers

The next forbidden practice found in Deuteronomy 18 is "charmers."

What are charmers? First, perhaps we need to define "charms" to better see what a charmer does. The *Merriam-Webster Collegiate Dictionary* defines the word "charm" as:

> Word Date: 14th century
> 1) a) the chanting or reciting of a magic spell: INCANTA-
> TION; b) a practice or expression believed to have mag-
> ic power
> 2) something worn about the person to ward off evil or en-
> sure good fortune : AMULET

A "charmer" is described below.

> Word Date: 14th century
> 1) a) to affect by or as if by magic; to practice magic and
> enchantment: COMPEL; b) to please, soothe, or delight
> by compelling attraction <charms customers with his

suave manner>

2) to endow with or as if with supernatural powers by means of charms; also: to protect by or as if by spells, charms, or supernatural influences

3) to control (an animal) typically by charms (as the playing of music) <charm a snake>

We have all seen or heard of mystic snake charmers from India. They play flutes alluring deadly cobras to dance and sway, tempting a viper bite that has meant certain death for centuries. We presume that there is more going on in these rituals than just the cobra either liking the music or deciding to end the life of his serenader. This is a chess game of spirits inspired by Hindu occultism. Knowing that Satan always counterfeits the good things of God, we can find a similar story in the Bible to back up the thinking that indeed spirits are involved in Hindu snake rituals.

In 1 Samuel 16:23 we read that David, instructed by God, played his harp and in so doing, evil spirits departed from King Saul. The life of Saul shows many similarities to that of a cobra as well. His unpredictability and destructive temper are particularly telling—just as a cobra.

Charms are all about superstition. Charmers promote charms and cast spells, supposedly to bring good luck or bad. For example, baseball players wear the same cap every day and go through the exact same series of events leading up to each game if they're on a hitting streak. Basketball great Shaquille O'Neal eats the same meal every day if he's on a scoring streak. Perhaps you've known someone who wouldn't step on the cracks in the pavement or who would immediately throw a pinch of salt over his shoulder should some be spilled while cooking or eating. Others throw pennies into fountains or make wishes on the stars. And then there is the complimentary fortune cookie, given after every meal in Chinese restaurants. These are all superstitions that have no basis in Christianity but rather display one's dependence on luck instead.

Many people carry charms to protect them. In a Christian bookstore we purchased a "pocket angel," an angel cut out of a penny. The accompanying card says:

> The angel in this penny is cut there just for you, seeking your safekeeping in everything you do. With the angel comes a prayer asking all be well, and too that God assign a sentinel to forever watch over you. May this guardian guide over you and keep you safe from harm, providing constant vigilance and protection in its arms. Put this coin in your pocket to remind you someone cares, constantly thinking of you, keeping you in their prayers. Should one day Heaven's gate require a key to unlock it, may you be found first in line with an angel in your pocket.

Another charm that people use for good luck are trolls. Some people actually think they are cute, but there is nothing in the troll legend that says that they are cute or bring good luck. According to northern European legend, trolls are called incubus spirits, which are spirits that materialize as men to have sex with women in their dreams. Do you really want something with that historical lore in your home, let alone in your child's possession?

Though you would think that less educated people, living in pre-civilized times, would have been more superstitious, people continue to be very superstitious today. A lasting superstition that most everybody is aware of is that most hotels do not have a floor numbered thirteen. Does anybody out there really believe that the fourteenth floor is not in reality the thirteenth floor anyway? Does that change it at all? Some people walk around with rabbit feet to protect them. (We presume the rabbit didn't think that foot was too lucky.) Others refuse to walk under ladders—rabbit's foot or not! Still others hold some spooky significance to Friday the thirteenth. Besides being a series of gruesome horror movies and a second rate TV show, any Friday that falls on the thirteenth day of the month is just another day.

Thankfully, luck or fortune have nothing to do with the life of a Christian. Or at least luck *shouldn't* play a part in our lives. "Lady Luck" is very seductive and has an evil master guiding her actions—the Devil himself. If Satan can convince us to depend on mere luck, then where does that place the Holy Spirit? Our worldview must include the knowing and assurance that God is in control and cares about every single detail—from the greatest to the least—in our lives. In Psalm 34:7 God promises:

> The angel of the LORD encampeth round about them that fear him, and delivereth them.

In Psalm 91:11–12 we read:

> For he shall give his angels charge over thee, to keep thee in all thy ways. They shall bear thee up in their hands, lest thou dash thy foot against a stone.

There are heavenly creatures working and protecting on our behalf—alleluia! Knowing this, what need could we have for a trinket fashioned by man, whether it be a pocket angel, a rabbit's foot, or any other lucky item or charm? What you need is the assurance, peace, and confidence that only comes from a rock solid relationship with God. Surely, the steps of righteous people *are* ordered by the Lord—by Him and Him alone (Psalm 37:23)! With our faith and our trust in Him we can rest assured that He is truly making all things work for our good (Romans 8:28)! Can any occult charm offer that?

Chapter 8

Forbidden Practice #7— Consulter with Familiar Spirits

The seventh forbidden practice found in Deuteronomy is a "consulter with familiar spirits."

Easton's Bible Dictionary defines "familiar" as follows:

> The word "familiar" is from the Latin *familiaris*, meaning a "household servant," and was intended to express the idea that sorcerers had spirits as their servants ready to obey their commands.

A "familiar," as they are known in the occult, is biblically identified then as an evil spirit or devil (i.e., demon or *daimon* in Greek). *Strong's Exhaustive Concordance of the Bible*: defines "spirit" in this usage as "an evil angel or demon."

A person who communicates with and seeks information from demonic forces is therefore a "consulter of familiar spirits." Such is the case of Saul and the witch at Endor from 1 Samuel chapter twenty-eight.

> Then said Saul unto his servants, Seek me a woman that hath a familiar spirit, that I may go to her, and inquire of

her. And his servants said to him, Behold, there is a woman
that hath a familiar spirit at Endor. And Saul disguised himself, and put on other raiment, and he went, and two men
with him, and they came to the woman by night: and he
said, I pray thee, divine unto me by the familiar spirit, and
bring me him up, whom I shall name unto thee.

—1 Samuel 28:7–8

There was no doubt that Saul, knowing full well that what he
was about to do was totally contrary to the commands of God,
went to Endor to get knowledge from the familiar spirit that
possessed the witch there. The Bible records that Saul's situation quickly turned from bad to worse. First, he abandoned
God, followed his flesh, and in his desperation, turned to evil
spirits. Then, just as he had been told at Endor, he and his
sons met their death as a result of Israel's defeat at the hands
of the Philistines.

This is a prime example of someone who became disobedient to the Lord's commands. Saul had ignored the Lord's
directive concerning the complete annihilation of Amalek
(1 Samuel 15) and thus lost the protection and leading of the
Lord. Rather than turn to God in repentance, instead he went
looking for knowledge in forbidden places, and in fact in-
curred the ultimate wrath of God. We surmise that just as
Saul did, untold millions have first become disobedient to
God and then sought counsel through occult means, followed
at some point by their demise. The moral here is clear. It
never pays to consult with demons, visit psychics, follow a
horoscope, or even attempt to operate in any realm of the
occult—never.

Are You "Familiar" with UFOs?

Wherein in time past ye walked according to the course of
this world, according to the prince of the power of the air,

the spirit that now worketh in the children of disobedience.

—Ephesians 2:2

We want to take this opportunity to speak to the enormous fascination and confusion resulting from the ongoing craze about Unidentified Flying Objects or UFOs. Nearly every day we hear increasingly about supposed UFO activity, alien beings, and their alleged interaction with and even abduction of humans. Reports of visitors from other worlds now permeate our society. Once relegated to the pages of sensationalistic tabloids or fantasy novels, suspected UFO activities are now reported about during the world's most respected newscasts. During recent times, nearly every newspaper and television magazine program have discussed UFOs and aliens. Radio personality Art Bell became one of the most listened to hosts in history by dedicating multiple hours each night to the discussion of UFOs and the paranormal. Mainstream wire services abound with articles on the subject, asking questions like, "If Aliens Visit Earth, Will They Be Friendly?" and "Speak Up ET! Thanks to NASA, If You're Out There, We're Listening." The sheer numbers who now report sightings have become dramatically more frequent. Though credibility may be questionable in some cases, and regardless of NASA's lack of official comment, more than one astronaut has acknowledged that they have actually seen alien craft while in space.

During the last twenty-five years, UFOs have allegedly been sighted over nearly every major city worldwide, as well as over military bases and nuclear sites. From the rural backwoods to the main streets of our cities, sightings of unexplained phenomenon in the skies continue to mount. Entire city populations have witnessed UFO events that local governments could not explain, most notably a saucer-shaped UFO which hovered over downtown Mexico City in broad daylight, producing thousands of eyewitnesses in July of 1997.

Pictures and video of that sighting were broadcast around the world. To this date, the much-reported event remains unexplained. It is no wonder that recent polls indicate that a majority of Americans believe that extraterrestrials most likely do exist. The study of UFOs or ufology has now become an obsession for multiple thousands, perhaps millions of people. All of this has contributed to the U.S. government spending millions of tax dollars trying to contact aliens.

Until 1954, only ten thousand people claimed that they had seen a UFO. However, it was around this time that the number of sightings skyrocketed. On November 29, 1973, a Gallup poll reported that fifteen million Americans had personally seen UFOs. Senator Barry Goldwater believed he saw a UFO. Boxer Muhammed Ali and Prince Charles both say they saw UFOs. Actor William Shatner claims that his motorcycle stopped in the desert and UFOs led him to safety. Even former president Jimmy Carter claims to have seen a UFO. Christopher Columbus reportedly saw UFOs four hours before he discovered America in 1492. And then there was the highly publicized sighting that guitarist Jimi Hendrix believed he had at the Woodstock Pop Festival in 1968. However, we surmise in Hendrix's case that what he thought he saw was probably induced by the LSD he had taken! But what about the millions of others?

Perhaps for us the most impressive barometer of just how expansive the study and discussion of UFOs has become happened during the writing of this book. While researching, we went to the World Wide Web and entered the term "UFO" into the powerful Inktomi search engine, which gleans prospective web sites across the Internet according to any desired search term. The results were staggering. As of mid-July 2000, the Inktomi search engine, which supplies Yahoo, AOL, MSN, Canada.com, and other search engines and directories with data, recorded a whopping **428,405** Internet web sites with information on UFOs! And that is just a partial figure, for the technology used in search engines normally picks up only the sites where embedded keywords actually reflect the exact term being searched for, such as "UFO"! Truly, the phenomenal interest surrounding UFOs has reached uncanny proportions today.

Alien Public Relations

Perhaps Hollywood's spotlight on the topic has done more to further the UFO craze than any other single thing. Obviously, there has been a constant stream of motion picture and television programming built around outer space, beings from other worlds, and space travel. Leading the way were movies like *Close Encounters*, *Alien*, and *Star Wars*, as well as the extremely popular television and movie series "Star Trek" and "The X Files." And of course the blockbuster, *ET: The Extra Terrestrial*.

Over the years, the improvement in the quality of Hollywood's presentations has truly been staggering. Great advancements have been made since the early days of *Buck Rogers* and *Flash Gordon*. Now, the electronic age has brought with it the capacity to blend ultra-surrealism with near absolute believability in recent box office hits such as *Armageddon* and *Independence Day*. Coupled with the state-of-the-art theaters of today, filmmakers have been able to employ ingenious electronic special effects, making powerful presentations that have deeply impacted viewers. While the special effects may be phenomenal, Hollywood's "magic" has left an unmistakable effect of a different sort on the lives of many people. The line between fantasy and reality has become more blurred with each passing year. The realism and tremendous effects leave the impression that there is at least a possibility that what one is viewing *could* be reality. Adding to this is the volume of actual real-life news reports concerning the very things that are now also supernatural subject matter for the big screen. Through news coverage, in books, and in particular Hollywood's capitalization on the subject, there is no doubt that a psychological conditioning of the culture concerning the possible existence of UFOs and alien beings has taken place. However, the question remains: What would we do if and when a UFO should land on the White House lawn? What reaction would Americans have to such an event, let alone a hostile attack such as depicted in Orson Well's classic radio play and subsequent motion picture *War of the Worlds*?

Have there been government cover-ups intended to shield us from knowing the truth? Are there really alien beings being held by our military deep in the Nevada desert at the secretive base known only as "Area 51" or elsewhere? Was there really a UFO crash and subsequent news blackout at Roswell, New Mexico, in July 1947? If so, who piloted the ill-fated craft, and where are the remains of the occupants today? Are we really being visited by beings from outer space? Or are we experiencing an elaborate, well-orchestrated brainwashing in an attempt to make us *believe* we have otherworldly visitors among us? If so, why and by who?

What Do YOU Believe?

Here are four scenarios that cover the UFO question.

1. **UFOs are a hoax and do not exist.** There has undoubtedly been some hoaxing through the years, but the overwhelming weight of evidence suggests that there are indeed vehicles or crafts in our physical reality that are unexplained, thus Unidentified Flying Objects.

2. **If UFOs exist, they are man-made and merely a part of secret military operations, testing and refining secret technologies around the world.** This possibility exists also and certainly could be the case in some instances. But again,

the evidence seems to suggest that nothing mankind has invented could be responsible for the majority of the sightings to date.

3. UFOs exist and are piloted by beings from outer space. Questions abound if this is the case. Are they just here observing us? Are they friendly? Or will they eventually become hostile? Are all of the UFOs sighted from the same planet or galaxy, or do we have multiple civilizations visiting us simultaneously?

One would think that if aliens actually desired to make contact, that we would have at least one rock-solid, irrefutable close encounter of the third kind, complete with credible eyewitnesses and proof to substantiate it beyond question, before the military could seal off the area and deny everything. If they actually wanted to make contact with us and really are of superior intelligence, wouldn't you think that by now they would have figured out that the best way to do so is to actually appear and land in a populated area—not Roswell, New Mexico, or Sedona, Arizona? This rather diminishes the argument that New Agers have advanced, which states that aliens are here to teach us and help us stave off elimination as a race. As a New Age author or leader, wouldn't it do wonders for your ego (and probably your checkbook as well) to believe that otherworldly beings have picked *you* out of the over five billion inhabitants of earth to communicate their still–secretive agenda to?

We can deduce as well that if alien beings were casing earth for a possible takeover, they would have likely made their move by now. If they can come from other worlds, it stands to reason that their technology, and presumably their intelligence, could overpower us quicker than you can say, "Take me to your leader." No, it appears that so far UFOs have purposely eluded mankind for the most part, being revealed only enough to let the mystique and speculation build to unprecedented heights. We believe this is no accident.

Note that evolutionists and atheists could theoretically line up with any of the three possibilities above, but could never agree with our last scenario, which is the one these authors believe.

4. **UFOs are not from another galaxy.** It is our personal belief that the UFO/alien phenomenon is one hundred percent inspired and engineered by Satan. They are actually demonic materializations in a very well orchestrated plan to deceive mankind and condition him to accept the supernatural in the end days. Thus, any alien beings that have been sighted or communicated with are demonic in nature. In fact, we believe in the very real possibility that aliens/UFOs could play a defining role in either events surrounding the explanation of the Rapture of the church and/or the subsequent rise to power of the Antichrist. We are not alone in this belief. Some of the greatest Christian minds of this century, including Dr. Walter Martin, thought the same.

The Identity of Aliens

In examining the UFO and alien phenomenon from both a biblical and New Age point of view, there are striking parallels. Though New Agers do not regard alien beings as demons, the information that some New Agers claim to have received from them certainly substantiates our belief that the Bible identifies these previously Unidentified Flying Objects and their occupants.

First, if you wish to study UFOs, you need to visit the occult section of your local library to find information. This in itself should be a tip-off. There you will find books with such titles as *Science and the Paranormal: Probing the Existence of the Supernatural, Creatures from UFOs,* and *The Supernatural from ESP to UFOs.* A perusal of the Internet shows the same mixture of UFO and occult information on many of the same web sites as well. In fact, the array of web pages that correlate New Age beliefs, the occult, and UFOs is blatant and staggering. For example, one web site advertised itself as follows:

> This site contains a huge amount of New Age and Spiritual information including Astrology, Wicca & Pagan, UFOs & ETs, Ascension, Earth Changes, Channellings, Crystals, Dreams, Divination, Angels, Magick, Karma, Meditation, and Healing.

Another said: "Channeling, Reiki, new-age, metaphysics, Feng Shui, angels, chakras, spirit, Bortner, masters, healing."

Still another ad said: "New Age Web Works Supports and informs the New Age, UFO, Pagan, Occult and Alternative Spirituality communities."

If aliens really are coming from other planets, why are they so closely linked with the occult? Why would occultists and New Agers have a corner on the market in communicating with aliens, if indeed they were actually from another world? The answer is simple but often ignored. The occult is about one thing—power from or communication with the spirit realm. Though most New Agers believe that aliens have chosen them to communicate with due to their spiritual "enlightenment," that's not really the case. What has actually attracted these beings who claim to be aliens is the proclivity New Agers have for spiritualism and other occult practices. Occultists and New Agers are versed in communicating with the spirit world—exactly where these "aliens" originate. So associating UFOs, aliens, and the occult together is for us a no-brainer. The outgrowth of the UFO phenomenon is doctrinally rotten. It lines up again and again with the world of the occult—not with God's Word. If for no other reason, this is why we believe these "aliens" to be nothing but masquerading demonic intruders who are weaving a deceitful web in order to further trap millions today. Even without integrating biblical understanding we see that both New Agers and UFO researchers concur, that there is indeed reason to believe that UFOs actually originate from another dimension and not from other planets or galaxies. Jay Allen Hynek, probably the world's foremost expert on ufology, said: "I do not believe they are coming from another planet. I believe they are coming from a parallel reality." We believe the parallel reality he is referring to would be the non-three dimensional supernatural realm described in the Bible. Entertaining this idea should be no quantum leap for the Christian. After all, Scripture reminds us that the Devil *IS* the "prince of the power of the air" (Ephesians 2:2) and the "god of this world" (2 Corinthians 4:4). Plus, we have instances throughout Scripture where angels appeared and operated in the natural physical realm in which we live. Let us remind skeptics for example that angels came to Abraham to announce Sarah's pending pregnancy (Genesis 18). They also came to Sodom and led Lot to safety (Genesis 19). And an angel appeared at the tomb of Christ announcing that He was risen to the two Marys (Matthew 29). In the first two instances, the angels were presumably dressed in the garb of the time and ate human food. And they all communicated in the earthly languages of those they met. This harmonizes perfectly with the warning we are given in Hebrews 13:2 to be careful to entertain strangers for they could be angels. All of this biblical evidence certainly gives good explanation as to how UFOs and their occupants could indeed maintain prolonged physical materialization. To magnify his plan for this age, Satan could, will, and does use many means to deceive his prey. He is the father of lies and illusion and his leash seems to get a bit longer with each passing day as we race toward the climax of the church age and the Tribulation to follow. That plan includes UFOs.

In her 1979 best-seller, *Aliens Among Us*, Ruth Montgomery broke new ground within the New Age community by laying out a case for the idea that some "humans" had evolved beyond the point of being born or going through childbearing. She believes that these beings who have come from "beyond the veil" are actually living as humans here on earth. She deemed these ETs "walk-ins." Millions say they've had past life experiences, which seems to verify the concept of reincarnation, so why not the belief that you were previously an alien life form? Sound far out? Well, there are a number of Internet web sites, some very intellectual, some very weird, that advertise themselves as touch points for these "walk-ins" to meet and share ideas and experiences. The first line on the back of Montgomery's book reads: "Prepare to meet our wondrous gods from beyond the earth." In researching "walk-ins" we found it interesting that the common denominators appear to be a belief in angels, UFOs, and the occult. To us, this is just one more confirmation that aliens and demons are one in the same.

Your Papers Please . . .

There remain several unanswered questions concerning UFOs. First, to our knowledge, there has never been a UFO gathered on radar coming into our atmosphere. They have been tracked many times while in our atmosphere, but they have never been detected coming *in* from outer space. How do they just come on the scene from nowhere? With all of the many dishes and antennas scanning space today, wouldn't you think that if these crafts were from outer space someone would have detected one approaching our planet?

How do aliens live and operate in our environment without any special aid? Are we to ignore all we understand about the other planets in our own solar system and instead believe that the aliens visiting us have just conveniently found an atmosphere (ours) with the right density and ingredients so as to support their life forms? Granted this does not take into account all of the biological possibilities, but it still bears asking.

If there are thousands of sightings, why aren't there more crashes? Knowing the ratio of air accidents in the world today, one would think that space aliens traversing earth's atmosphere and gravity would have provided more than the few *alleged* crashes which have produced no documentable proof. (If you were Satan and were trying to decoy mankind into believing in space creatures, you'd probably want a couple of *supposed* crashes to add to the folklore and mystique.) Think about it, if UFO sightings had always been a regular phenomenon, we'd have taken them for granted, just as we do the ability to look up and see a jet flying miles above the earth. This way though, the awe and mystery stays intact, but the reality stays conveniently just out of our grasp.

UFOs—The Mask of Satan

Why have these aliens traveled perhaps trillions of miles anyway? Just to pester people? You would think, if they were traveling that far, that they would have an agenda, a purpose for coming here. Also, if you've watched much *Star Trek*, you've been taught that these visitors cannot alter human history. We'd like to know just who made up that rule? Under Satan's direction, these charlatan space aliens may someday alter the entire future of mankind. Certainly, they are having an adverse effect on those who have crossed paths with them already.

A close encounter of the first kind is when a person sees

an unexplained object. A close encounter of the second kind is when aliens leave some sort of evidence, such as the charred remains of an animal or perhaps an authentic crop circle. A close encounter of the third kind is when someone actually comes into physical contact with an alien, such as in the case of an abduction. Those who have had close encounters of the second or third kind have noticed a strong stench of sulphur in the vicinity, just as in the movie *The Last Starfighter* when the smell of sulphur denoted the presence of aliens. Anyone schooled in deliverance knows that among other distinguishable signs, the stench of sulphur is one of the calling cards of demonic activity. Another parallel is that UFOs rarely appear in daylight. They usually come after dark when the temperature drops. The Bible says that those who follow evil love darkness rather than light. If you have ever been around a séance, during the actual contact with the spirit world, there is usually a strong sulphur odor and the temperature in the room falls. We can tell you from personal experience that when demons are present, during exorcisms for example, the air turns a strange cold.

Every time someone is abducted into a UFO, they seem to always be given some kind of sexual evaluation. The usual aftereffects prove to have devastating consequences. Here are some of the by-products that seem to be consistent with those who have had a close encounter of the third kind.

- They have had severe psychological problems, even insanity.
- They have had severe sexual problems.
- They have lost their families and jobs.
- They have become reclusive.
- They have gotten involved in some kind of cult.
- They have gotten involved in the occult.
- They have committed suicide.

Does any of this sound appealing? Of course not, yet mankind continues to be like a moth circling around a candle. Instead of flying away to safety, eventually it flies right into destruction. With us, instead of turning to the Lord, our fallen nature outside Christ steadily draws us into Satan's arms.

Angels and Demons

Some within New Age circles have surmised that UFOs are actually the vehicles of angels. We think not. It is important for our study to examine and define these spiritual creatures.

We have no biblical record of angels of the Lord ever possessing people. Have you ever heard of someone being "angel possessed?" No. The Bible says they are "ministering spirits, sent forth to minister for them who shall be heirs of salvation" (Hebrews 1:13). Most of their assistance seems to take place from the invisible spirit realm, but as we've mentioned, there is ample evidence that they do materialize and operate in the natural world on occasion. We don't have an overwhelming amount of scriptural evidence about them, but we do know that God's angels act for the good, on behalf of the Christian believer.

Most theologians believe that demons are fallen angels, and though there is some discussion about this, we know that in his deceptive and cunning manner, Satan persuaded one-third of God's angels to follow him in prideful rebellion against God. Thus they were banished and cast out of heaven. If indeed fallen angels and demons are one in the same, then in their present state, they have the ability to actually possess people. They carry out the antithesis of what God by His Holy Spirit does. He first fills and then leads Christian believers. Demons, when given the opportunity, can "fill" (possess) and then manipulate the lost. In mentioning this, we recognize that there is great consternation about whether a Christian can actually be possessed by a demon or not. We do not believe so. However, we fully believe that a believer who has "chinks" in his armor can be subject to demonic oppression and depression. Secret sin robs the Christian and can render both his prayers and the protection of God somewhat ineffective and, as we have said, we become targets for trouble when we walk from underneath God's protective wings (Psalm 91:4).

In the New Age movement today there is a lot of discussion about angels. This biblical concept is a mainstay in New Age culture. However, as we have pointed out, New Agers reject words such as "demon," "Satan," or "hell" as "old-fashioned" and "antiquated." This is the "cut-and-paste Bible" syndrome, electing to pick and choose what biblical information they will receive and what they will ignore. In a quest to codify their religion, New Agers and occultists have opened themselves up for angelic visits that are actually demons circling like vultures.

Crazy for Angels

If you've watched many of the daytime talk shows, especially *Oprah*, you are aware of the current angel craze. A whole parade of authors and a whole lot of books are expounding on angels and their interaction with men, but with one important element missing—historic, biblical foundation. Isn't it odd that the religions that inspired and taught man about angels, Judaism and Christianity, are only mentioned in passing as stories of enlightenment through angelic encounters are bandied about with only one corroborating criterion—experience.

The intense spiritual hunger being exhibited in our society is perhaps most evident in man's latest quest to be "touched by an angel." While these authors enjoy and are encouraged by the television show of the same name, and while it may bring a certain amount of balance to the angel craze, it needs to be made crystal clear that of the thousands of accounts of personal supernatural angelic experiences being reported, the vast majority are not of God. There are two common factors present with virtually every spokesperson pushing an "angel" scenario. First, they are not Christians, but have had some sort of supernatural experience with an entity claiming to be an angel. And second, the angel has become like a personal savior to them who supplies spiritual enlightenment. Considering the Bible's admonition for us to use God's Word to test or "try" the spirits (1 John 4:1) and to test all things and reject anything that doesn't line up (1 Thessalonians 5:20–21), how can a non-Christian, who doesn't yield to the authority of Scripture, have any clue what is coming from God or what may be of the Devil? Simple—they don't! The only litmus test that people have to go on is something which the Bible expressly warns us not to trust by itself—human experience and intellect. Bible believers know the Lord's instruction well: "Trust in the LORD with all thine heart; and lean not unto thine own understanding. In all thy ways acknowledge him, and he shall direct thy paths" (Proverbs 3:5–6). But how is a nonbeliever to discern an angel of God from an imposter? Because of the increasing spiritual void in the end times, great numbers of people are finding themselves emotionally and spiritually attached to things that *sound* good and *seem* somewhat similar to the religion of their parents or grandparents, but it is in reality as deadly as a cobra bite.

The Cost of Angel Worship

Many New Age materials encourage us to meditate with angels; however, the practice is found nowhere in Scripture. In Eastern mysticism, meditation means to empty oneself in order to be filled by an outside force. In Christianity, prayer and meditation are the avenues to be filled with the Holy Spirit through the Word of God. Other New Age materials tell us that angels would like to be a part of our lives, and instruct us on how to contact our angels. There is nowhere in Scripture that instructs us to inquire of angels.

Nick Bunick, a millionaire, insists that he is the reincarnation of the apostle Paul in the book *The Messengers: A True Story of Angelic Presence and a Return to the Age of Miracles* by Julia Ingram and G. W. Hardin (Simon & Schuster, 1998). A billboard advertising campaign for the book touts: "The story the angels want told." It ought to say: "The story Satan wants you to believe!" Bunick's angels, who espouse reincarnation, are *not* angels of the Lord. The Bible teaches nothing about reincarnation. Once again, it is a demonic substitute for salvation and the resurrection. This book has had a tremendous and deceptive impact on many people. While researching this book, we found the following comments from the publisher on the Barnes & Noble Bookseller Internet web site (*barnesandnoble.com*).

> Nick Bunick was confronted by angels, and it will change your life forever. . . .

> Nick Bunick gives back to us angel's messages spoken two thousand years ago when Jesus walked the earth. These messages are as true today as they were then: Within every one of us is a part of GOD. It is that which gives us life and it is that which is everlasting. If we but look within, our own love will fashion a new and compassionate world.

"Within every one of us is a part of GOD. . . . If we look WITHIN . . ."??? That's not what the Bible teaches! No doubt, this book is pushing a New Age version of Jesus and a misleading nonbiblical account of angels. It all sounds so inviting to the untuned ears of those who don't know what the Bible actually says.

In 2 Corinthians 11:14–15, we read as the Scripture speaks directly of the origin of Bunick's story and countless others today:

And no marvel; for Satan himself is transformed into an angel of light. Therefore it is no great thing if his ministers [fallen angels] also be transformed [or appear as] the ministers of righteousness. . . .

Readers who had purchased the book at the Barnes & Noble site had entered some opinions about it. One reader praised the book saying:

This book changed my life and will change anyone's who will read it with an open heart.

Another stated:

I originally bought this book for my mother who was very intrigued with Billy Graham's "Angels." I decided to read it first and once I started it I couldn't put it down. I have always felt the bible (sic) was too literally translated in several areas.

Still another, identified only as an "uneducated religion seeker" wrote:

I totally found this book helpful in learning more about jesus (sic) and the reason we are all here. It has helped me to understand religion better than any church has tried to teach me in the past.

Oh, Lord help us! Only one reviewer on the web site wrote from a biblical viewpoint and questioned Bunick's authenticity as Paul's incarnate and his account of what these "angels" imparted to him.

Our hearts sank as we read these reviews for another reason as well. The New Age has sprung up because we have let down with the truth. The spiritual death and confusion emanating from many who preach the liberal gospel of "self" (all the while claiming it to be "Christian"), breath the infection of theological liberalism into the lives of millions each week. We who know the truth that sets men free **must** make the gospel simple and powerful at every opportunity. The Devil has blinded so many spiritual seekers, sidetracking them onto his dead-end called the "New Age." Help us, Lord! Help us to expose the enemy's traps and pull people out of the fire before it's too late!

Paul writes to Timothy about this very condition again saying:

> Now the Spirit speaketh expressly, that in the latter times some shall depart from the faith, giving heed to seducing spirits, and doctrines of devils.
>
> —1 Timothy 4:1

The angels that are appearing to New Agers today are not talking about the almightiness of God; they are talking about how great they are, and they are seducing people to worship them.

Angel worship is commonplace today. The Bible speaks to false, idol worship many times and speaks directly to this in Colossians 2:18.

> Let no man beguile you of your reward in a voluntary humility and worshipping of angels. . . .

Perhaps God's most vivid warning concerning this is in Exodus chapter twenty.

And God spake all these words, saying, I am the LORD thy God, which have brought thee out of the land of Egypt, out of the house of bondage. Thou shalt have no other gods before me. Thou shalt not make unto thee any graven image, or any likeness of any thing that is in heaven above, or that is in the earth beneath, or that is in the water under the earth: Thou shalt not bow down thyself to them, nor serve them: for I the LORD thy God am a jealous God, visiting the iniquity of the fathers upon the children unto the third and fourth generation of them that hate me.

—Exodus 20:1–5

How strong the Lord's words are! The words ". . . have no other gods before me . . ." and, "[worship] no likeness of any thing that is in heaven" are some of the most powerful words ever spoken to man! To do so will bring the sin of idolatry on your children's children and their children! This is indeed serious stuff and again, the only criterion for those following angels is human experience. This must seem like a picnic to Satan!

Do We Believe in Angels?

As has happened so many times while writing this book, we have uncovered instances in our ministries and lives that are uncannily parallel. Here is another example. In David's own words read of what may have been a true angelic encounter.

Recently, while traveling through Pennsylvania with my family, I lost control of my car when I hit a patch of ice. On one side of the interstate was a forty-foot drop to the other lanes of oncoming traffic. On the other side was a snow-covered embankment covered with trees. When my car came to rest, we had landed backward in the embankment and had not received one scratch. About a half-mile ahead of us were two men in a truck who came back to help. They didn't say very much—just inquired if we were okay and helped us get the car out of the embankment, and then they went on their way. We never saw them again. Were we "touched by an angel"? Maybe—I don't know—but I do know that I didn't praise the angels (if that's what they were) for helping us. I thanked God for sending them in our time of need.

Eric and his wife Melanie experienced nearly the same thing years ago in Idaho.

We had been driving through the mountains of eastern Oregon in a blinding snow most of that Saturday. Slowed considerably by the storm, we knew we would have to drive nearly all night to make it to central Idaho where I was to speak in a local church the next morning. I was sleeping in the back of our van and Melanie was driving. We had been at a snail's pace the whole trip but now the intense snow was turning to rain as we descended the east slopes of the Blue Mountains. At least Melanie **thought** it was rain. What she couldn't see was the sheet of ice forming across the road before her. Nearing Caldwell, Idaho, suddenly, the rear end of the van began to swing wildly back and forth. All I remember was hearing Melanie scream "JESUS!" as we slid sideways and off the road. I was able to scramble out of the rear door of the van and around to the driver's door. We had stopped head first in the ditch just a few inches from a fence. To our right was a grove of trees and to the left a fifteen-foot embankment. But we had stopped between them, and short of the fence. Incredibly, after we composed ourselves and consoled our dog, who had been thrown onto the floor from the seat he was asleep on, I was able to back the van out of the ditch and back up onto the roadside!

However, when I attempted to drive away, we had absolutely no traction and began to slowly slide sideways toward the middle of the freeway and the cement "jersey" barrier. Now, we were completely sideways blocking both lanes of traffic. Thankfully, we knew that no one was going to be driving by at sixty miles an hour, but it was harrowing anyway. Though I tried and tried to get us headed in the right direction, I couldn't push the van because it was so slick. I couldn't get a foothold for traction with my feet.

The moments seemed like hours, but lo and behold, here came a police car! I know they are employed to patrol, but what brought these two policemen down this deserted freeway at four a.m. in such horrible conditions neither they nor we could explain. In just a moment they had pushed my van around so I could drive down the edge of the road and then off the exit about a mile away. We watched as the policemen got back in their car and drove away unimpeded.

Both of us have remarked since then that we believe they could have been angels assuming the posture of policemen. Regardless, we just know that the Lord sent us some very timely assistance out there, be it human or angelic! And remember that was in the days before cell phones, too! We were stuck on a deserted stretch of road in a very precarious position and one way or another, God sent us help.

In addition, I have always wondered if I had looked close enough, would I have found heavenly fingerprints on our vehicle which would have evidenced why we missed the fence, the trees, and more ominously, the cliff. Each time our ministry travels take us over Interstate 84 just inside the Idaho border, I will forever think of that spot as the place where the Lord sent His supernatural servants to our aid.

End-Time Messengers

Why are these aliens coming now? The buzz about them is no mistake. There is an unparalleled intensification of spiritual activity going on. There is no doubt a very powerful and persuasive conditioning process underway. Leading psychologists tell us that if humanoids were to appear today, more than likely the world would accept them and possibly make messiahs out of them. As certain as some are that UFO abductions are real, we are witness to how Satan is currently using the aroused interest in UFOs to destroy lives and capture souls. A Roar market research poll released in December 1999 reported that nearly twice as many British youths believed in ghosts and aliens as believed in God. But Satan has more up his UFO sleeve than just turning part of those in our society toward a false belief in UFOs. We are in the midst of watching one of Satan's most masterful plans in action as he desensitizes mankind about the supernatural, preparing them for what is to come. All of this is working in concert to fuel a new but demonic interest in spiritual things. As we have presented, there is no doubt that man is fast becoming addicted to spiritual things. But just as the Father of Lies has planned, these spiritual things are not leading people to or coming from God.

This is all leading up to a moment in time when the church of Jesus Christ will be "caught up" to be with Him in the clouds. Though the Rapture will be the most immense "UFO" event in history, Satan's years of promoting and purveying UFOs, supernatural beings, and the occult all come to bear on how he will manipulate and gain the confidence of mankind through his henchmen, the Antichrist and the False Prophet, as foretold in the Book of Revelation.

When millions of people disappear simultaneously, somebody had better have a very good explanation. Here are two scenarios on what might take place immediately after the Rapture. First, either the Antichrist or UFOs directly will come forward with this message: "There have been millions of people who have been stolen away by an evil force. The people of this force walk like us and talk like us, and the only way we will know who you are is if you have our mark."

The second scenario could be that the Antichrist will announce that all of the "narrow, bigoted Christians" have been taken away by our "friends" from space to be reprogrammed. Now that the Christians are gone, the earth can heal and the "Age of Aquarius" can dawn. This scenario fits what Madam Helena Petrovna Blavatsky (the nineteenth century Ukrainian spiritualist and founder of the Theosophical Society which spawned today's modern New Age movement) taught, as well as other New Age authors such as Alice Bailey and Marilyn Ferguson. Regardless, the post-Rapture world will be in tremendous upheaval. Besides the emotional strain of loved ones and business associates going missing, the financial turmoil will be staggering. Just imagine taking, let's say, one billion people off the planet in the twinkling of an eye. Brother, you've got a complete financial collapse and total physical chaos everywhere!

It Simply Comes Down to This
Our discussion of UFOs, aliens, and angels boils down to this one point. If any being—no matter how good; no matter how supernatural; no matter how awesome—should appear and then *not* declare that Jesus Christ is Lord and the only way to be saved, that creature is straight from the pit of hell.

Beloved, believe not every spirit, but try the spirits whether they are of God: because many false prophets are gone out into the world. Hereby know ye the Spirit of God: Every spirit that confesseth that Jesus Christ is come in the flesh is of God: And every spirit that confesseth not that

Jesus Christ is come in the flesh is not of God: and this is that spirit of antichrist, whereof ye have heard that it should come; and even now already is it in the world.

—1 John 4:1–3

It is our task to test the spirits as Scripture admonishes. And one thing is certain, if we are wrong about the alien/demon relationship and if there *are* indeed any beings from other planets visiting us, they will also be subject to the Almighty God of the universe who hung the stars they've traveled from, the same as we are.

Chapter 9

Forbidden Practice #8— Wizards, Magicians & Sorcerers

It is rare in today's culture to hear someone refer to himself as a "wizard." Though the term is used quite a bit in talking about someone's abilities, the connotation is not one leading to the occult.

But Hollywood and the television industry continue to ride the occult to the bank like a Halloween witch to a séance!

The scene was set. The "white" wizard (the good guy) is set against the "black" wizard (the evil guy). It's a classic case of evil vs. good, right? Not so fast. It seems that the hero wizard, the head of a clan of up-and-coming wizards, is using incantations and spells, the same as the villain character. Both use the name "Beelzebub" to energize their occult spells and prayers. And both draw from the same mysterious power, one doing so for evil and one contending it is for good. Only the intentions of their minds and the end results they seek are different, for the occult power they tap promises to work for both sides—and it does.

As the plot thickens, the evil wizard searches feverishly for the camp of the good wizard and his flock. Once the evil wizard finds them, the good wizard must cast an incantation against him to erase his memory of the experience.

The pentagram, perhaps the most powerful of occult symbols, adorns the set continually. Evil images appear and transcend from it when even the "good" wizard casts his magic spells. It's an occult tug of war. Back and forth they go.

What we are describing is a very popular and long–running television program. What is it? Would any Christian parent ever allow his or her children to watch it, let alone buy them the products associated with it? God forbid. Yet, it happens every time the *Smurfs* cartoon is broadcast!

Smurfs is one of the most watched cartoons in history. Its popularity was and still is worldwide. The program was produced for broadcast in at least twenty-five countries and several languages. To our shock, we found over **thirty thousand** web pages on the Internet covering the Smurfs (30,728 to be exact)! Frankly, it's like a cult of sorts. There are web sites that play Smurf music and Smurf video clips and even a group of anti-Smurf sites that ridicule all the sites that endorse the Smurfs! Weird!

As this book goes to print, the cartoon is currently playing five days a week on the *Boom Network* found on American cable and satellite systems. The array of toys, games, and books produced with the Smurf logo and images continue to play in the imaginations and memory banks of millions of kids and now even young adults worldwide.

Papa Smurf is perhaps the most infamous wizard or sorcerer of our time. Holding true to the realism presented through television and motion pictures today, the word "smurf" itself even means "little devil." Each week for over twenty years, Papa Smurf and his adversary, Gargamel, the evil wizard, hold court to introduce white and black magic to our kids. Azreal, the name given to Gargamel's cat, seems to come from a Hebrew word which means "helper of god." But where is God in this? Absent.

We may never allow our children to watch an occult laden TV show or so-called "slasher" movie, but it is perhaps the more innocent shows that are our biggest concern. At our seminars, parents sit back and "amen" us when we talk about the worst in today's entertainment. However, when we mention some programs or toys such as the Smurfs or the old cartoon "My Little Pony" (which both of us took lots of heat for a few years ago because we saw mysticism and mythology in the plot and characters), the "amens" turn to uncomfortable frowns. But the truth is the truth, and the occult doesn't always have a horrific face painted on it. It matters not that it's "white" magic against "black." It is one hundred percent occultic! It's the Devil's work and it's produced from his camp with but one idea in mind. No, actually three ideas . . . to kill, steal, and destroy.

Chapter 10

Forbidden Practice #9— Necromancy—Voices from Hell

The ninth forbidden practice is "necromancy"—communicating with the dead.

We have discussed séances and channeling all through the book, but for all of you "spot" readers, we'll define this again.

Channeling is the occult (now New Age) practice of lending one's mind and body to the spirit world to be used in communicating with the dead. This same thing has transpired during séances for centuries. But in our time, the twist is that the channeler now speaks as if it is actually the deceased person or entity being contacted who is doing the speaking. It is as if the channeler's mind, body, mouth, and even hands (in the case of "automatic handwriting") are taken over for a time while the spirit from beyond uses it.

This practice has become wildly popular and has gained acceptance because of the high visibility many influential people, including Hollywood stars, have given it.

Because of the tremendous yearning that Hollywood has displayed for New Age spirituality over the past three decades, there has been an exponential rise of those trying to accommodate the fervor. Most saw Vincent Price as quaint, eccentric, or just plain odd, so when he produced a recording of "readings" entitled *Witchcraft and Magic: An Adventure in Demonology*, no one really took it too seriously. But we now know that Price was serious, having an affinity for not only his persona as Hollywood's leading man of the macabre, but for the actual subject matter itself. Whether disregarded as just another performance of the role that gave him notoriety or not, the album included a track called "How to Communicate with the Spirits" which amounted to nothing more that an advocation of necromancy.

Hollywood's Occult Craving

In the 1970s and early '80s few mediums claimed to be an actual physical voice or channeler for particular spirits from the dead. Mediumship had been a matter of contacting someone's departed loved one or perhaps a famous figure from history and merely reporting what the "spirits were saying." Channeling, with the accompanying trance-state of altered consciousness, was going to take contacting the spirit realm to another plateau all together.

Though it was still a little discussed practice, one that few stars would admit delving into, it became obvious that fame, fortune, and popularity did not satisfy the inner self of Hollywood's elite. While mediums still had to weave their way to the star's doorsteps through a sort of occult underground, the craving for spiritual enlightenment for those in the entertainment world became public knowledge in the 1980s. When Shirley MacLaine released her book, *Out on a Limb*, in January of 1984, it cracked the dike in Hollywood's secretive silence concerning New Age and occult practices. Soon star after star paraded forward to give homage to either their channeler or the spirit whom they had come to trust.

As if growing in the fields adjacent to Los Angeles, channelers and mediums began to pop up like bean plants in summer. When Sharon Gless of the popular 1980s TV series "Cagney and Lacey" won the first of her two Emmy awards for best actress in 1986, she thanked Lazaris, her spirit guide, for the award. As it turned out, Lazaris was also the first spirit we know of that employed an agent to promote "it"! Mafu, another popular "spirit guide" to the stars, was channeled through Penny Torres, a Southern California housewife. Mafu claimed to be a member of the "Brotherhood of Light." Joyce DeWitt, of "Three's Company" fame, brought this particular spirit to prominence. Others followed into the mystical realm such as Lily Tomlin, Philip Michael-Thomas, Burt Reynolds, Sylvester Stallone, Stephanie Powers, and Tina Turner, to name a few.

Perhaps the first prominent channeler of our time was Jane Roberts, a housewife from Elmira, New York, whose use of the Ouija board initiated her journey into the occult. Roberts and her husband began searching for spiritual answers and to their surprise the entity they came to know as "Seth" spoke back to them through the Ouija. Over the next two decades they recorded and chronicled over fifteen hundred experiences with Seth. Having turned away from Christianity and to Eastern mysticism due to bad experiences while in a Catholic school, Roberts began compiling the "Seth Materials" in 1963 and continued until 1984 when she died. During that time, Seth channeled a total of twenty-three books (totaling over six million volumes sold) as well as several tape series and interviews through Roberts. The 1972 best seller *Seth Speaks* catapulted Roberts into the national spotlight. Springing from the relativist theme that all humans actually create their own reality based on their personal beliefs, the

"Seth Materials" have been called the "Blueprint for the New Age" and rightly so. Roberts work continues to this day through Seth Network International headquartered in Eugene, Oregon. As of the year 2000, Roberts' widower, Rob Butts, 81 (who still uses a Ouija board!), is compiling and releasing between eight and ten new volumes of Seth materials comprised of the first five hundred and ten sessions which Roberts had with Seth.

Unquestionably, the most famous channeler of our day is J. Z. Knight. This housewife from Washington State has developed an empire from the financial proceeds of thousands of followers. Ramtha's School of Enlightenment has touched thousands of "truth-seekers" with the deception of the enemy and attracted several lawsuits from disgruntled followers and their families in the process. Those who have journeyed from around the world include an assortment of dignitaries and jet setters. Actress Linda Evans, of TV's "Dynasty," even moved from her Southern California mansion to the small community of Lakewood, Washington, to be near Knight's headquarters in the lazy farming community of Yelm. Perhaps more notable, though, is the fact that for the first time, a spirit guide, Ramtha, has gained even more name recognition than its channeler. Throwing Knight into altered states, jerking and contorting as it delivers its New Age messages through her in a man's voice with an English accent, Ramtha claims to be a thirty-five thousand-year-old Lamurian warrior. Now honestly, doesn't it take a whole lot more faith to believe that than to trust in the eyewitness account that Jesus lived, died, and rose from the grave to save mankind? At least we have actual proof of what the Savior did and said!

Several New Age cults have sprung forth from the channeling movement, most notably Elizabeth Claire Prophet and the Church Universal and Triumphant, headquartered in western Montana. Prophet's teaching centers on communicating with and for a hierarchy of spirits known as "ascended masters." (Please note the New Age connection with the West Coast of the United States. From Mount Shasta in northern California to Vancouver, B.C., Canada, we find what appears to be the highest per capita concentration of New Agers in the world.)

We also need to again mention the much publicized escapades of First Lady Hillary Rodham Clinton, who has for years depended on the guidance of a spirit claiming to be that of deceased former First Lady Eleanor Roosevelt

Necromancy—Voices From Hell

One of the reasons we are warned against the practice of necromancy is because though a person might *think* he is communicating with the dead, this is actually not the case. Remember the story of the rich man who died and went to hell in Luke 16:19–31? He wanted to communicate with his brothers to warn them, but was unable to because of a void fixed between departed souls and living humanity. Either Jesus was telling the truth in this account or He was a liar. New Agers can't have it both ways. They can deny the existence of hell all they want, which is the central reason reincarnation is so appealing, but it doesn't make it any less real. Instead of conversing with the departed, those who practice channeling and mediumship are actually contacting demonic familiar spirits who are masquerading as the deceased, for Jesus (whom many New Agers say they revere) taught that no one (not even Abraham) was able to impart information from the grave.

What we said earlier concerning how psychics operate, making those seeking their counsel marvel at their knowledge of personal or public history, applies here. Demons feed channelers information packaged as if it is actually coming directly from someone deceased, when in reality what is transpiring is a demonic version of the trade employed by such famed impressionists as Rich Little or Dana Carvey. Though channelers in trance states may actually *sound* like the departed and may have *knowledge* that someone now deceased possessed, it is merely a demonic ruse to trap those willing to seek help or information in Satan's forbidden territory.

Channeling's Number One Doctrine—Reincarnation

Spirits speaking from beyond the grave continue to extol that they are products of reincarnation cycles. As we've mentioned in the chapter dealing with astrology, reincarnation is not taught in the Bible. However, spiritual seekers with no solid foundation to delineate truth from error will often grasp *anything* forwarded from the spirit realm. In a quest for purpose and meaning in life aside from the Bible, millions are believing the age-old lie of the enemy, "ye will be as gods" (Genesis 3:5). The logical conclusion of reincarnation is "spiritual enlightenment and fulfillment through a system of works." It teaches that eventually we end up at the pinnacle of a spiritual hierarchy with no need for physical bodies, entering what the New Age refers to as "ascended mastership."

Some people believe that Jesus verified reincarnation because in John 9:1–3 we read:

> And as Jesus passed by, he saw a man which was blind from his birth. And his disciples asked him, saying, Master, who did sin, this man, or his parents, that he was born blind? Jesus answered, Neither hath this man sinned, nor his parents: but that the works of God should be made manifest in him.

The disciples' question here displays two erroneous misconceptions. One is that all sickness or infirmity is due to the direct result of sin. The second is that the man's sins may have somehow caused his blindness. If indeed it did, this would open the door for one to surmise that he could have had previous lives, for the Scripture records that he was blind since birth. But to believe either of the misconceptions the disciples mention here, you must disregard the complete counsel of the rest of the Word of God on the matters of afterlife and also sin. Still, New Agers have jumped on this verse, contending that the disciples' question and Jesus' lack of direct response correcting them does indeed sanction reincarnation. The fact is, many in Jesus' day believed in reincarnation. There was obviously a lack of sound, scriptural teaching available as the Jewish leadership had disintegrated to primarily figureheads. (Remember the amazement people constantly displayed at the teaching of Jesus?) The disciples had yet to come to grips with sound theology on this and many other issues. Jesus, being the master apologist of heaven, chose to let their question go by, just as He does concerning other matters throughout the four Gospels. Speaking only what was necessary, as was His habit, Jesus saw only the need to deal with healing in this passage. Though the alleged reincarnation inference is an interesting question, it fails to pass the test of sound and complete biblical understanding. This should be viewed as a perfect example of why it is dangerous to graft a single scripture from the Bible to attempt justifying a doctrine that the weight of biblical evidence denies.

If reincarnation is actually sanctioned by God, then why is it that we have yet to read of an account of a channeled entity speaking forth that Jesus Christ is God and the only way to be saved? One would think that if reincarnation were indeed true, at least one of the thousands of documented cases of channeling would have claimed to be of an orthodox Christian speaking from the grave. Instead, all we ever hear from the channelers is that Jesus was a great teacher but that the Bible is just another religious book and one need not expressly follow it, for there are many paths to God. But if the spirits speaking actually *did* endorse reincarnation as from God they would have to contradict this powerful passage in Hebrews 9:27–28.

> And as it is appointed unto men once to die, but after this the judgment: So Christ was once offered to bear the sins of many; and unto them that look for him shall he appear the second time without sin unto salvation.

Oh, beloved, make no mistake; He *IS* coming back again, but not in a reincarnated form. As this passage states, His first time here paid the price for all our sins. The purpose of His second coming will be to translate His church out of this world and on to glory!

Let us further address what we said concerning the story of necromancy with King Saul and the witch at Endor (1 Samuel 28) back in chapter eight. This instance has always been one surrounded in controversy. Was it *really* Samuel speaking from the grave? Whether the entity that spoke to Saul was a demonic spirit masquerading as the deceased prophet Samuel or whether it was actually Samuel speaking from beyond is unclear. God may have allowed the latter in this unique situation just as He stopped the sun in the sky *just once* in Joshua 10, etc. He is God, and within the boundaries of His Word, He can do whatever He desires to accomplish His purpose. Regardless of who was speaking, Samuel or a demon, the tragic outcome and God's disdain for this occult activity is clear. It is also certain that one would have no grounds to build a doctrine on this one unique event either. Regardless of who was speaking through the witch at Endor, the New Testament—which supersedes and fulfills the Old—powerfully teaches resurrection instead, and never once teaches practices such as necromancy or praying for the dead. Instead, it encourages talking regularly with a risen Savior!

We're so grateful that God did not institute a system of karmic birth and rebirth for us to atone for our own failures and sins. Instead, He sent His beloved Son to once and forever pay the price for the sins of Eric Barger and David Benoit. Otherwise, we'd be living in this life to pay penance for the failures of the last and would have to come back again to fix what we fouled up in this one. Oh, how wonderful is the depth of His plan and love for us!

Part Two

Doorways to the Devil— Entertaining Spirits Unawares

Chapter 11
Enemy Infiltration

For the LORD thy God walketh in the midst of thy camp, to deliver thee, and to give up thine enemies before thee; therefore shall thy camp be holy: that he see no unclean thing in thee, and turn away from thee.

—Deuteronomy 23:14

Beware lest any man spoil you through philosophy and vain deceit, after the tradition of men, after the rudiments of the world, and not after Christ.

—Colossians 2:8

It would be shocking if we could look into the lives of Christians to examine what exterior influences and practices are the reasons they aren't achieving the spiritual victory that Jesus won and God intended them to have. The fact is, whenever we volitionally invite the wrong influences, images, activities, conceptions, or thoughts to have safe harbor in our lives, we are short-circuiting God's plan for us to be "more than conquerors" (Romans 8:37). Instead, God's Word demands that we stand up against and expose the many deceptions the Devil is foisting on society (Ephesians 5:7). Opening a door to allow the three enemies of mankind—the world, the flesh, and the Devil himself—to infiltrate our lives and homes can be devastating. We've pointed out that the consequences of ignorance are just as severe as those brought by willful disobedience. So, as part of the well-balanced Christian life, we must take responsibility to instruct our households about not only what God takes pleasure in, but also what He abhors.

Recognizing spiritual battlegrounds in our culture and society is one of the most important tasks for the Christian today. We are now going to discuss some of the more unsuspecting battlegrounds of Spiritual Warfare today.

All or Nothing?
Some readers may be surprised why we bring up some of the specific issues that appear in the subsequent chapters here. From our many years of ministry in this area, we know that for some individuals there may be a partial failure in seeing the reasons why we find some of these issues important to our study. We don't want to assume that each reader is on the same "wavelength" with us, so to speak, for we know that is certainly not the case. We are acknowledging this in hopes that those less accepting of our viewpoints might look at the topics we're going to cover in the next few chapters with open eyes. A classic example of what we are referring to is illustrated in why we found it necessary to examine the Smurfs in chapter nine.

Though the cartoon has been airing since the late 1970s, and though other Christians, such as our friend Phil Phillips (*Turmoil in the Toybox*, Starburst Publishing) have done sparkling exposés concerning it, there is still a large disconnect in the Christian community when Satan's work comes in "cute" and "innocent" packaging. Our point is that Christians are not to make decisions based on what the culture deems good or bad. Nor are we to accept the "lesser of two evils" as acceptable on a sort of "moral slide rule," while staying clear of the "really bad stuff." God's Word clearly lights the path that leads to righteousness and, in turn, to His wonderful peace and bountiful blessings. But He gives us the choice as to whether we'll follow Him or our flesh and cultural pressures.

Others would be shocked if we *didn't* mention some of those things outlined in the following pages. There will be a few who believe we should simply just ignore the entire world system, throw away our TV sets, and turn off our minds to what is happening around us. While we are tempted to climb up on the roof and pray for the Rapture at times too, this viewpoint is unrealistic and certainly gives way to the fallacious thinking that "ignorance is bliss." True, we are to live in the world but not of it. However, if we are unable to dialog about the sensations of Satan in the day in which we live, how will we ever successfully communicate our reasons for abstaining from them? Just as when dealing with the cults, we have to do better than throw a tract at them and simply tell them Jesus loves them. If we are to be effective in dialog and witnessing to them, we must have some idea of what they have come to believe in and be able to share why we believe what we believe. The same is true in communicating God's truth about the culture as a whole—including its various entertainment mediums and characters.

The television, VCR, and today's technology in general are not the problem. They can be used for good as well as evil. The problem lies in the heart of man. For many of our fellow Christians, it is a problem of self-control. For some, the particulars of what they entertain themselves with is not the stumbling block. Instead, the battle is with simple time management. God has been given a backseat to hour after hour of harmless yet spiritually fatal recreation. Fatal because we have allowed it to rob us of time—time that God longs to spend with us in prayer, worship, study, and Christian service.

We battle with these issues in our hearts and homes just like you do. And let us be quick to add that we aren't preaching some sort of sinless perfection or heavy works doctrine to you as if we have no failings. So please don't take this as a guilt trip, inferring that we have it all together and others don't. As husbands, parents, and ministers, if we aren't in a constant state of growth, openness, and repentance before the Lord, we have lost sight of the truth we seek to proclaim. Finding a biblical balance, upholding righteousness, and yet trying to avoid falling into the trap of legalism is precarious and certainly not easy, both in our ministries and personal lives. But the point is simply this. Instead of walking in either of the two extremes of surrendering to the onslaught of media and allowing our families to be audience to everything under the sun or doing the opposite by attempting to cut off all entertainment or communication with the culture, there is another solution. By making the volitional decision to abstain from evil, yet understand its workings and effect in the culture, we position ourselves to be more potent for and blessed by the Lord. This position allows us valuable inroads making it possible to have dialog with those caught on either of the extreme sides we mentioned. We believe the biblical position is to take on the world system and what it promotes head first, waging warfare with the influences, doing our best to lead as the Holy Spirit leads us, and teaching those entrusted to us how to deal with its traps and pitfalls as we go. Though we cannot live our kid's lives for them, we have been given an awesome responsibility to direct them in the right way. If we shirk this, we guarantee there is a plethora of Satan's workers dressed like rock stars and entertainers who *will* teach them.

Whadda 'Ya Mean That's "Evil" . . . ?

It is amazing to us how many people we talk to in our travels who say they are Christians but who either refuse to or just don't understand the need to filter what they allow into their lives. We've heard defenses for nearly every occult practice, cult group, rotten TV program, "R" rated movie, satanic rock star, and demonic plaything over the past decade and a half of ministry. Sometimes it becomes almost comical—sometimes not. Besides those with far out ideas on the fringes of Christianity, our public ministries have attracted the likes of witches and cultists, who have come to our seminars to disrupt us when we've spoken out against witchcraft, Satanism, and the occult. One Sunday night, as Eric addressed a church in Oregon concerning the occult parallels of Freemasonry and Mormonism, a member of the lodge stood up near the back of the church and began to swear at him! You can imagine this caused more than a little stir in the audience! Though the pastor was going to have him physically removed from the church, Eric quietly lobbied that he be allowed to stay. There is much more to this story, but the public confrontation and resulting conversation after the seminar resulted in the man giving his heart to Christ the next morning. (Praise the Lord!) This is not totally uncommon. Though neither of us asked for the ministry of stirring up the proverbial demonic hornet's nest wherever we go, experience dictates that the most uncomfortable situations we face often result in the greatest victories for the Lord.

With Heads Firmly Planted in Sand . . . (On Satan's Beach!)

After carefully laying out our case night after night in local churches, continually citing Scripture, and laying out compelling and well-documented evidence, almost invariably it happens. Someone walks up afterward who either didn't get the picture at all or who finds it necessary to argue against what to us are clear and overwhelming biblical precedents. We've wondered sometimes, "Was this poor person even here for the seminar, or did they just read a flyer and show up after the service?" In some cases, these have been unbelievers who mistakenly think that we are advocating a complete abolition of their culture. (So-called "reconstructionists" believe this.) No matter how balanced and biblical we try to make our presentations, there are going to be people who either cannot grasp or really just don't want to accept what we are trying to say. When it comes to analyzing the Christian worldview as opposed to the entertainment culture surrounding us, Satan is well equipped to deafen the ears, blind the minds, and harden the hearts of some so they just can't delineate what we are saying or why we are saying it. Talk about a spiritual battle!

It would have been easy to give up and get discouraged, to look for another field of ministry that drew less fire, or to just leave God's work completely. But we just simply can't. Not only have we found great joy in those who *have* been set free by what the Lord has shown us to do, but He sent us on a mission that seems to have no opt-out clause. He has sent you on it, too. Even though Scripture prophetically promises that the world will indeed grow darker as we move through the end days, that hasn't changed the command to lift up Jesus and biblical principles one iota.

Just like many others in our line of work, both of us have endured everything from letters signed in blood, to angry witches having to be physically restrained, to telephone death threats, to angry rock music fans coming *en masse* to our seminars to mock and cause trouble. If we couldn't handle the heat, we'd have both gone fishing permanently by now, but in so many of those cases, we were merely presenting facts and ideas that had never been heard by our listeners before. We were viewed as the enemy, when in reality we were actually telling them truths that could save their lives, both physical and spiritual. However, when the world, the flesh, and the Devil are involved, it's usually hard to hear things that are diametrically opposed to your longtime, well-entrenched belief system.

We're Big Boys . . . We Can Take It!

The topics we've concentrated on during our public ministry are no doubt lightning rods which attract the ire of many. Eric's book, *From Rock to Rock: The Music of Darkness Exposed*, was a Christian bestseller in 1990–91. However, many secular interviewers ripped into him from the first moment of an interview to the last because he was exposing their sacred cow from the inside out. It didn't matter that Eric's background was based right in the middle of the rock music world. It didn't matter that he had been a record producer and a drug addicted musician almost all his life. What right did he have to say such things about such talented musicians?

Being that both of us have devoted major portions of our past ministries to the study and discussion of secular rock music, we have been grilled time and again by interviewers bent on proving us to be a couple of wackos. In fact, that's how we first met back in 1985 when a Seattle TV station happened to book us both to appear on a program about the influence of rock music in the culture. The show was slanted from the outset and portrayed us as two wild-eyed, religious, right-wing fanatics, which was then and still is the norm for the secular press to do. We were undaunted and stood our ground but left the studio knowing we had both gained a friend for life. From that very first day we knew we were a perfect match! (It's amazing that it has taken us fifteen years to finally write a book together!)

Though we haven't actually ministered together all these years, our seminars and ministries found a somewhat similar niche. One thing we've talked about from time to time is how people have constantly misconstrued what we believe. For example, our critics have insisted that we believed that listening to rock music would send a person to hell, yet neither of us have ever once said that and do not believe it. Instead, our concern has always been concentrated on the lyrics and the lifestyle presented by the secular musicians of our day. The secular music scene is just not biblically conducive nor an atmosphere where Jesus is glorified. Even rock fans have to admit that after a few hours of listening to the artists of today, you really don't feel much like praising the Lord and going to Bible study! However, year after year our secular counterparts have continually tried to skew the issue, disingenuously making people *believe* that we are saying something totally different.

We've always contended that the music and entertainment someone partakes of are choices, pure and simple. Nobody is being forced at gunpoint to listen to or watch anything. Yet the opposition just doesn't want anybody coming along questioning the perverted and satanically based value system adhered to by today's entertainment world. The same was true when dealing with witches and Satanists as well.

Not many witches endorsed David's book *Fourteen Things Witches Hope Parents Never Find Out*! For the most part, the secular and New Age world just cannot come to grips with a worldview built on moral absolutes. What's more, they certainly cannot stand negative exposés about the practices, lifestyle, or products of those they admire from the world of music or entertainment. Regardless, this is what the Lord has called us to do and in this, we will continue. How else will people, in particular the kids of today, be given both sides of the story? We suppose it's kinda like the saying, "It's a dirty job, but somebody's gotta do it."

Now, have we written all this in an attempt to somehow draw sympathy from the reader? No, not at all. We are recounting these experiences to make the point that standing by the truth and holding to biblical principles—in the face of direct opposition—is not an easy task. It isn't for us and it won't be for you. The world around us disdains it and many in the church would rather ignore doing it, but we view it as absolutely essential if we are to enjoy the level of spiritual victory that Christ levied for us at the cross. And so far, we have not nearly received the kind of treatment that Paul and Barnabas did in Acts 14.

Remember the story there? Having just fled the persecution of both the Jews and the Gentiles for presenting the Word of God at Iconium, Paul and Barnabas traveled to the "peace and safety" of Lystra. There, they preached and as Paul was speaking, his eyes met those of a man who had been crippled since birth. Being led by the Holy Spirit, Paul commanded the man to rise up, and as he did, he was completely healed! Upon seeing this, the people began to deliriously declare that Paul and Barnabas were "gods." This immediately caused Paul to rebuke the crowd and carefully preach the truth about who God really was. This, however, did not win him any citizenship awards or commendations. Instead, Paul and Barababas were stoned and left for dead outside the city gates! The same spirit is at work in our world today. Even in the face of great miracles, the religious world (including the occult) does *NOT* wish to be told the truth. It is much more desirable to misconstrue, misrepresent, or outright reject something that one doesn't want to accept and then lambast either the message or more likely, the messenger.

When you know the truth that will set men free and you've been called to present it—even if it's a constant fight—you've just *gotta do it*! The mission of the Holy Spirit isn't usually to make us comfortable in the hearing of the truth. It is quite often the exact opposite, for God desires us to change and be transformed into the image *HE* is looking for, not the one that we have grown accustomed to.

Though we've never been stoned for our messages and have never endured the intense persecution Paul, Barnabas, and many other Christians throughout history have, both of us understand their zeal, motivation, and frustration. The Bible tells us that Paul and Barnabas returned into Lystra the very next day and then came back again sometime later (Acts 14:20–21). In the face of opposition from both the pagan religionists who worshiped false gods and the Jews who were out to stop them, Paul and the other disciples were undaunted in their mission to declare the truth. Paul recognized that not only were he and God's other chosen soldiers in a physical struggle to present the gospel and expose the darkness, but that those physical struggles were actually a direct result of demonic hostility. The only answer for them was to forge on! He wasn't about to allow Satan to succeed. If we are to achieve victory in our lives and homes, we must dig in and do battle to ***disarm the powers of darkness***—just as Paul did! We encourage you to do likewise as you resist the enemy's evil infiltration at any cost.

Chapter 12

Now a Word From *Their* Sponsor—Satan!

Here we're going to list just a few examples of television, cartoon, and movie programming that have been used in the ongoing inoculation of our world concerning the occult. The media, with very few exceptions, ignores any Christian content portraying Christ's victory through the cross. Anything goes but Christ. Previously in the book we have given much of the theological explanation and occult information and definitions that apply to the selections in this chapter, so we'll just detail the various programs and movies unless further explanation is warranted. We want to point out the fact that so many of the programs and movies we'll discuss here are animated. Experience tells us that adults tend to often make less critical choices with them and more readily allow children to view them uninhibited. This is a mistake. Our children and grandchildren are soaking in the values system being portrayed. Remember as well that kids are not nearly as sensitive about watching the same show or tape repeatedly as adults. Thus, the mother of teaching—repetition—comes into play much more dynamically with them.

In preparing this chapter, we could have picked any of hundreds of examples. These following examples are meant to just illustrate the magnitude of entertainment portraying occult and supernatural themes. We have tried to pick some classics, some current TV and movie examples, and some cartoons to make the point. However, the most important thing to remember when making choices about what you and your family will or will not watch is not what we did or did not single out. The most important element is for you and us as the Lord's chosen people to follow His written standard which transcends what Hollywood or the networks may come up with in the future. Following biblical understanding must take precedent over cultural popularity.

Please note that you may want to refer to this chapter when attempting to dialog with people who are either un-knowledgeable of the Christian viewpoint or who think that Christians, who have problems with the witchcraft and occult influences in our culture, have either lost touch with reality or have just had too much caffeine!

Media "Make Believe" Makes Believers!

Bewitched. Thirty years ago Elizabeth Montgomery portrayed Samantha, a "good" witch, in this extremely popular TV show. "Bewitched" is still seen today on the popular Nickelodeon Network. The obvious inference of white witchcraft with Samantha and the slightly more devilish (no pun intended) attitude of her mother, Endora, is obvious. (Note the biblical reference to the witch at Endor, 1 Samuel 28.)

This show broke new ground for television, giving witchcraft a half-hour, prime-time spotlight each week. It taught us to do more that just tolerate witchcraft. It promoted it, encouraged it, and above all worked subtly on our senses teaching us to adore it.

Sabrina, the Teenage Witch. This current weekly ABC

TV series portrays a young, cool witch who uses supernatural powers to attain what she wants. Each week Sabrina and her talking cat, "Salem" (remember Salem, Massachusetts?), deliver the goods for the Devil. The "cute" look of its predecessor, "Bewitched," is now replaced by this show with an edge on it. A quick look through current publishing databases also turns up at least two different book series spun off from "Sabrina," one aimed at children and one advertised for teens.

The ABC.com web site described the August 4, 2000, episode as follows: "After Sabrina is grounded for breaking curfew, a magic prospector zaps her to the Wild West, where, as the new sheriff, she happily declares a formerly rule-ridden town rule-less." Need we say more? This is a perfect example of how entire segments of the entertainment world of today are fulfilling the warning of Isaiah 5:20–21, calling evil good and good evil and becoming wise in their own sight!

Charmed. Following the popular trend of witchcraft themes, actresses Alyssa Milano, Shannon Doherty, and Holly Marie Combs star in this weekly Warner Brothers show about three young, beautiful, and feuding sisters who have an ancestry in witchcraft. The sisters, who've inherited their grandmother's San Francisco house, learn they came from a witch coven and quickly follow suit. Experimenting with witchcraft, they discover they've been targeted by various warlocks and other evil entities.

Buffy, the Vampire Slayer. To illustrate the kind of blatant promotion of occult practices and ideals, on the official Buffy web site (*www.buffy.com*), a section called "Slayspeak" claims to be a "handy reference guide to the lingo" and does an ample job at introducing readers to the occult—just as the Buffy movies and TV show have done.

Listed in "Slayspeak" are occult practices and terms such as:

astral projection—the theory that while one sleeps one has another body—an astral body—that can travel through time and space

feeding—drinking blood; a vampire's only means for survival

harvest—a night once in a century when a Master Vampire can draw power from one of his minions while it feeds

host—the person off whom the vampire feeds

master—the most powerful of vampires, capable of destroying the earth

minion—a follower of the Master Vampire

slayer—a girl born once every generation with the strength and skill to hunt vampires, find them where they gather, and stop the spread of their evil and the swell of their numbers

vampire—demonic creatures who live off the blood of humans; a vampire appears to be a normal person until the feed is upon them—only then do they reveal their true demonic visage

vessel—a minion, bearing a three-pointed symbol, which can give the Master Vampire power by feeding

watcher—person who finds the slayer and leads her on her path; it is his destiny to guide the slayer.

As foreign to our Western thinking and as rare as it may be, vampirism is not just a legend. But neither Buffy nor any other mortal has the tools to fight this or the other weapons in the Devil's arsenal. Without the anointing of the Holy Spirit and the protection of God, any efforts a human may make against the world of the occult is futile.

Beauty and the Beast. This popular children's story and accompanying movie and TV show portray the practice of lycanthropy—the ability to turn into an animal. Occult lycanthropy is where the idea of werewolves or vampirism originated.

In this movie, a woman falls in love with an animal. In *Beauty and the Beast*, the audience is aware that a spell had been cast upon the man, but Belle didn't know this and though she thinks she's in love with a man, she is actually in love with an animal. In the television series by the same name (not the Disney version), the two had sexual relations and produced a baby that was half human and half animal. This practice is known as bestiality. The Bible expressly forbids and condemns those who lay with animals, yet now it's associated with a popular modern-day icon.

It is interesting to note that in the Church of Satan, founded by Anton LaVey, church members put on their animal garments during particular satanic rituals. One of the constants in the Church of Satan is sexual perversion, so we can be assured that *Beauty and the Beast* could be on their "suggested viewing" list if they should ever produce one.

The Bible says that demons can possess animals. When the demons were cast out of the men in Matthew 8, they entered the bodies of swine, and the swine then killed themselves in the ocean. If a demon cannot possess a human, it desires an animal. If the circumstances make neither available, they desire any animate object that a human(s) may ascribe inordinate value to or worship of. Demons love idolatry, and throughout our ministries we've logged many occasions when *things* have been used by Satan to capture a victim. A great example of how people get drawn into the snares of the enemy is not the use of occult objects themselves, but rather an antique car. A story comes to mind of a teenager who ascribed such love and devotion to a car he had rebuilt that it had allowed Satan more than just a foothold. During a deliverance session, the demon that had plagued the young man indicated that he had a right to infect the boy's life. It was revealed that the teen had idolized his car so deeply that it had opened up the door for demonic possession!

Animorphs. We can't help but mention the *Animorphs* book series. In the *Animorphs* series, children are able to turn into animals. Scholastic published a booklet called *They're Coming: Everything's About to Change*, which is an introductory book for the *Animorphs* series. The whole premise of this series is to promote the idea that a person can change from a human into an animal. Isn't it interesting that evolution teaches that humans came from animals, and spiritism teaches that animals are superior to human beings?

Mighty Morphin Power Rangers. The Power Rangers are able to turn into animals. One Power Ranger is able to turn into a falcon, which was worshipped as a god in Egypt. Another is able to turn into a frog, which was also worshipped as a god in Egypt.

Captain Planet. In the opening credits of this cartoon for children, it is explained that five children from around the globe have been gifted by Gaia, Mother Earth, with one each of these same five elementals, and that when used together, these powers summon Captain Planet. The final words before the cartoon starts are: "The power is yours!"

Gaia is the earth goddess from Hinduism and has been popularized in the West by the expansion of New Age philosophies.

The Lion King. In Disney's animated hit *The Lion King*, Rafiki anointed the head of the central character Simba. In doing so, it is portrayed that no one can bring peace over the kingdom except someone ordained by witchcraft. In perhaps the most dramatic scene in the movie, Simba looks to the night sky and speaks to his deceased father, seeking guidance, and his father speaks back! It is very difficult to explain to a six-year-old child why that child can't talk with deceased loved ones, when Simba talked with his dead father. That is not a minor doctrinal error; that is one hundred percent demonic. As we've pointed out in chapter ten, that is called necromancy, and we are warned against it in Deuteronomy 18. This very popular movie openly taught and encouraged mystic and New Age beliefs to millions of children worldwide.

So Weird. Another Disney production. This one is a weekly TV show on the Disney Channel starring McKenzie Phillips. The basic story line of the program is that Fiona Phillips, or Fi as she is known (Cara DeLizia), is a fourteen-year-old girl who is a paranormal investigator. Fi's mom, Molly (played by McKenzie Phillips), is a seventies rock star touring across the country. Fi finds paranormal mysteries wherever they go. Plots include Bigfoot, aliens, angels, ghosts, telekinesis, etc. It's kind of an "X-Files" for kids. The "So Weird" link from Disney's web site is loaded with occult imagery and terminology. This show represents but one more promotion of the occult and paranormal to children and teens.

The X-Files. Perhaps the most popular of the paranormal–based shows in the past decade. Story lines run the gamut including any and every imaginable occult and UFO theme.

The Others. This prime time program from NBC features a group of psychics who examine paranormal claims and activities. The official NBC web site for "The Others" includes a lexicon of paranormal terminology and an online tarot card reading service inviting readers to "find out about their future."

The Sixth Sense. This is the horrific story of an eight-year-old boy who is tormented by his ability to channel the thoughts and wishes of ghosts. The 1999 movie won rave reviews and was a huge box-office success. We found it interesting that it was marketed with the chilling tag line, "Not every gift is a blessing." How true.

What Lies Beneath. This summer 2000 box-office hit stars Michelle Pfeiffer and Harrison Ford. The Christian based "Preview—Family Movie and TV Review" (*www.gospelcom.net/preview*) said this about the film:

Claire (Pfeiffer) . . . begins to hear strange noises and doors seem to open by themselves. Then she starts seeing images of a dead girl. And the girl seems to have some connection with Norman (Ford). . . . The film includes strong occultic images and even encourages occultic practices. When Claire tells a psychiatrist about her haunting encounters, he encourages her to try communicating with the spirit. She and a friend, who also purports to use psychics, try using a Ouija board. The friend later gives Claire a book about sorcery, which includes contacting the dead. The spirit even seems to possess Claire's body while she holds a lock of the dead girl's hair. Although the emphasis is on occultic spiritism, the film also includes some disturbing images of near drowning, bloody faces, and a decayed corpse. Necromancy, or contacting dead spirits, is condemned in the Bible and therefore, an unacceptable practice.

The Wizard of Oz. We know it's a classic, and we know that many readers will hold fond memories for it, but this is the classic story of white vs. black witchcraft. It broke ground for the many other witchcraft promotions Hollywood has produced over the past fifty years. It was one of the first movies to portray witchcraft as acceptable.

The Wizard of Oz brings us to an old analogy. How many of you reading believe that the public could have made the leap from Judy Garland in *The Wizard of Oz* to Freddie Kruger in *Nightmare on Elm Street* without a lot of desensitizing and time passing? The truth is that we as a culture could **never** have made that jump. We have been as a frog in the pan of cold water. Everything was fine, even as the stove was being lit. Things weren't too bad when the water was just a little warm, but by the time we realized what was really happening, we had become too weak to climb out and soon became the delicacy on the Devil's dinner plate. Just as a person who is poisoned just a little each day with arsenic doesn't die after the first dose, in the end after enough small doses, their organs begin to shut down and they are doomed. The same has happened to us morally in our culture and surely it is the same concerning the church's general lackadaisical attitude concerning witchcraft and the occult.

Pocahontas. In the cartoon-styled Disney movie *Pocahontas*, we find the same elemental spirits as in witchcraft—earth, fire, water, sky, spirit, etc. In this short exchange between the characters Grandmother Willow and Pocahontas, we find earth, water, spirit, and sky (astrology).

> Grandmother Willow: "All around you are spirits. They live in the earth, the water, the sky. If you listen they will guide you."
>
> Pocahontas: "I hear the wind."
>
> Grandmother Willow: "What is it telling you?"
>
> Pocahontas: "I don't understand."
>
> Grandmother Willow: "Listen with your heart."

Morning Glory Zell, a witch, had this to say about *Pocahontas:*

> It is without a doubt the most pagan-positive movie to ever come out of Disney, and is now alongside *Fern Gully* and *Captain Planet*, teaching kids why Mother Nature deserves our reverence and protection.

The Disney version of *Pocahontas* totally neglects the fact that Pocahontas became a Christian. Her baptism is so significant to American history that it is pictured in the Rotunda building in Washington, D.C. But in this historically perverse production by Disney, Pocahontas converts John Smith to pantheism (the belief that all is God and God is in all).

Teenage Mutant Ninja Turtles. In the late 1980s these pizza–eating kid heroes crawled out of a sewer, across the screen, and right into your child's heart. Led by their guru, a rat named "Splinter," they portrayed the role of their ninja namesake to our kids, which is "a feared paid assassin." After the release of David's book *Fourteen Things Witches Hope Parents Never Find Out*, a witch called David to protest his adamant stand against witchcraft. We found it interesting that at the end of the conversation she told David that she would never let her children watch "Teenage Mutant Ninja Turtles" because it was too violent. In this, she was right! At one time a few years ago, "Teenage Mutant Ninja Turtles" was rated the most violent program on television (by average acts of violence per moment)! We thought it was ironic that a witch won't let her children watch violence, and yet some Christians allow their children to watch anything they please.

During the height of the Ninja Turtle craze, the AFP wire service, Johannesburg, South Africa, reported the following on November 26, 1990.

> South African school children, influenced by the Ninja Turtle craze, have taken to attacking their parents with "turtle" weapons and their fellow pupils with sharpened sticks. Other children have been found slipping out of their homes at night and when confronted by worried parents, they said they were responding to "the call of the turtles." This came to light after a weekend rampage by three boys who fantasized that they were Ninja Turtles. Two of the boys involved in the incident were five years old. The other was eight. They told their friends that they were "Ninja Turtles run amok" and using axes and hammers they broke into a nursery school, breaking glass, ripped up floor tiles, smashed doors and cut up toys.

Anyone who thinks this is an isolated incident should think

again. When Eric was a boy he barely escaped serious injury while following the lead of an action cartoon (we think it was "Roadrunner"). Catapulting a brick into the air as he had seen in the cartoon, it came down, hitting him in the head, which facilitated a trip to the hospital for stitches and observation! That image is mild considering what is now being portrayed to our kids via cartoons, daytime, and even nighttime programming each week.

Freakylinks. In the fall of 2000, Fox TV is airing a new primetime program based on the escapades of a maverick web (Internet) journalist who investigates paranormal phenomena. The star (Ethan Embry) takes over his deceased brother's web site only to see him on the Internet! The show, aimed at teens, encourages exploration into the occult, is a product of the creative team behind the *Blair Witch Project* movie and drives viewers to visit one of the weirdest, occult-laden sites on the Internet.

The Little Mermaid. In Disney's *The Little Mermaid*, Ariel agrees to trade her voice to the demon, Ursela, in exchange for three days as a human.

Annie. This "family" movie included a character named Punjab who waves his arms and casts a spell on Annie's dog, Rusty.

Chapter 13

Parents Beware!
What's in that Cartoon?

Everyone knows that the greatest tool for teaching and instilling ideas is by using visuals. The eye gate probably produces the deepest mental impressions of any of our senses. This is why television has become such a vital vehicle for the social engineers today. Coupled with the power of stereo surround sound, television is unquestionably the most powerful teaching tool ever created.

A strange phenomenon takes place while watching television purely for entertainment. With our minds caught up in the storyline, the visual effects, the characters, and acting, we seem less able (or perhaps willing) to discern doctrine and values when they are being promulgated. If a news program is being watched or any sort of Christian programming that involves teaching, most of us carefully dissect the values, societal, or political impact, morals or doctrinal correctness of the content. But when we are watching something purely for entertainment, not only do our minds find diversion, escaping the cares of the day, our discernment also seems to become somewhat passive. Now we do not have any clinical studies or mass polling information to substantiate this. But, human experience and our years of ministry in this area tell us that while most Christians would not accept false doctrine or a lower moral code from someone's *teaching*, we more readily subject ourselves to such if it is packaged as *entertainment*. With all of this, we are referring to how adults assimilate and digest television. But for children, it is vastly different.

With our kids, television represents one hundred percent entertainment. Other than the restraints and guidance we give, they are prey for the values and morals being taught to them each day. This is not to discount the work of the Holy Spirit as He hovers over our children, but most parents will admit that the signs of original sin usually show up very early in a child's life. Still, regardless of how much it affects each child from one to the next, the fact is that at the earliest ages, values and morals are being taught to our kids in virtually every program they watch. In the view of the designer, children must not only be entertained, they must also be indoctrinated into political correctness, as well as doctrinal correctness. Political correctness is designed to instill humanistic teachings, while the doctrinal correctness indoctrinates the viewers into New Age and occult philosophies.

A close look at the themes of some programs aimed at adults and the majority of children's programming today, will indicate the work of a careful designer. Though they work on developing a program's characters, stories, or sets, the designer is not actually the programmer, technician, producer, or director. The designer is extremely versed in the images and script he wishes to promote. He knows how to get things done and is able to position the shows and movies portraying his desired values into prime locations in the viewing lineup. He has control over and is able to manipulate situations and the thoughts of many people in places of great influence in today's entertainment world. He has a vast network of unseen workers to facilitate his purposes around the world. They come from the spirit world. They are the demons. The designer's name is Satan.

The Scripture clearly illustrates this in Ephesians 6:12–13.

> For we wrestle not against flesh and blood, but against principalities, against powers, against the rulers of the darkness of this world, against spiritual wickedness in high places. Wherefore take unto you the whole armor of God, that ye may be able to withstand in the evil day, and having done all, to stand.

Manipulation of Our Minds

If you understand that Satan is the author of confusion, you will understand what part confusion plays in the scheme of things. An example of this may be to tell the public that we have a problem with teenage pregnancy, then show programs where children involve themselves with heavy petting and bedroom scenes.

Forty years ago we didn't have a national problem with teen pregnancy like we do today. Television programs like "Leave it to Beaver" never showed the parents in bed. In "I Love Lucy" and the "Dick Van Dyke Show," they had separate beds. Forty years ago, you rarely, if ever, saw two people under the age of eighteen years of age in bedroom scenes. The brilliant answer that the left-wing of our government has for this problem is millions of dollars for education and billions of dollars for abortion. Let us give you a current example of how the media is being used to manipulate our public mindset.

Why is it that government research has proven that having tobacco advertising at baseball parks or in magazines encourages young people to smoke? Yet, Budweiser's TV ads use funny frogs and slogans like "I really love you, man" that become instant catch phrases for elementary kids, without promoting underage drinking? "Joe Camel" and the Budweiser frogs would seem to appeal to the same audience, but few give the frogs a second thought. Why? Because they haven't been **told** to by the government and media. That statement may sound too simplistic and may even offend our intellect because it's our human nature to believe that **we** are in total control of our thoughts and mindset, but it's true.

We have been inundated with talk about the tobacco companies because particular people want the public to believe particular things at a particular time. Undoubtedly, the alcohol industry hasn't been targeted with forced redistribution of wealth, as have big tobacco and other corporations, such as Microsoft, who have refused to play along with government regulators. We wonder if the fast food industry will be the next mark for big government bureaucrats. After all, couldn't they surmise that millions of people are experiencing health risks, high cholesterol, and obesity because of the high fat content in a Big Mac or Whopper?

Regardless of the actual health risks, it is politically correct to oppose smoking. Tobacco companies, oil companies, and others have been villainized by a very focused campaign to do one thing—extract more money from them. While we oppose smoking (like most who read this book do) and while we disdain the legalized extortion that our federal government has been participating in, all this has happened through the use of a finely tuned publicity campaign to sway public opinion toward more governmental control. And as we all know, the government public relations machine has had great success. Our point is that through manipulation of the medium of television, the same kind of thing has been going on in much of today's children's programming as well.

There has been a shrewdly targeted campaign from hell

to manipulate children at the earliest age to accept witch-craft, sorcery, violence, rebellion, and immorality and to re-ject absolute morals, parental authority, and God. But in this case, few seem to be concerned or even aware of what is happening. Rarely has it been pointed out to the public that this is bad (except by religious zealots like us)! There's been no government inquiry into the promotion of witchcraft in children's programming. Because of the large profits, not only from the actual cartoons themselves, but from the extensive marketing of toys, books, videos, games, and clothing, etc., the flood of anti-family, anti-God programming aimed at chil-dren continues to grow everyday. You don't even have to watch the cartoons to find out that this is true. Just walk down the aisles dedicated to toys at your local Wal-Mart, Target, or K-Mart stores. Virtually every toy series is a spin-off from a pop-ular cartoon, the majority of which would have blown the minds of even secular parents from the 1950s, should they be catapulted through time into our day for a look. Still, the fact that these occult-laden products continue to sell as they do speaks to their popularity and also to the ignorance of the public about the potential negative impact on our children.

With that in mind, remember how closely kids emotion-ally relate with what they play with. Playtime is their occupa-tion and too often parents are completely disengaged about what their kids are ingesting, sometimes for hours each day. Just as with other habits of the flesh, what satisfies a child this week, won't next week. That's a frightening thought con-sidering the weird, occult, and violent fare that is currently shaping the fragile and impressionable minds of children each day. Though television moguls will try to convince the gener-al public that their products are but a reflection of society, in reality what they produce actually changes society. This axi-om will dubiously be proven never truer than in today's car-toons.

What's in that Cartoon?

As we travel, we are often asked to comment on different cartoons as both of us have ministered about and exposed the effects of Hollywood and entertainment on our culture for years. We thought it would be fitting and helpful to give a brief rundown of some of the children's programs available at the time this book was completed. We have devised a rating system to help you discern the content of some of the most popular cartoons today and also to open communication with your kids to discuss moral and biblical values with them and how it relates to what they entertain themselves with. You will also find this rating system helpful as you employ it with new programs as they are made available for your children. Though the cartoons may change and will generally continue to get worse than they are presently, this system will be a valuable tool as you seek to direct and shape your child's life and stand for righteousness.

Here is how the rating system works.

V=Violence

Jesus warned that as it was in the days of Noah so shall it be when He comes again. The rise of demonism produces a violent environment. Satan induces this upon a world following his ideals. He comes to steal, kill, and destroy (John 10:10).

The earth also was corrupt before God, and the earth was filled with violence. And God looked upon the earth, and, behold, it was corrupt; for all flesh had corrupted his way upon the earth. And God said unto Noah, The end of all flesh is come before me; for the earth is filled with violence through them; and, behold, I will destroy them with the earth.

M=Mythology

Mythology is based on the belief of polytheism. Polytheism is the belief that there are many gods and goddesses to be worshiped by and give aid to mortal men and women. Superstition and mythical literature have forwarded polytheism through the ages.

> For they said unto me, Make us gods, which shall go before us: for as for this Moses, the man that brought us up out of the land of Egypt, we wot not what is become of him.
>
> —Exodus 32:23

Paul got in real trouble when he came against the goddess of Greek mythology Diana.

> So that not only this our craft is in danger to be set at nought; but also that the temple of the great goddess Diana should be despised, and her magnificence should be destroyed, whom all Asia and the world worshippeth. And when they heard these sayings, they were full of wrath, and cried out, saying, Great is Diana of the Ephesians.
>
> —Acts 19:27–28

The Bible not only tells us there is one God, it tells us to reinforce it in our children's lives.

> Hear, O Israel: The LORD our God is one LORD: And thou shalt love the LORD thy God with all thine heart, and with all thy soul, and with all thy might. And these words, which I command thee this day, shall be in thine heart: And thou shalt teach them diligently unto thy children, and shalt talk of them when thou sittest in thine house, and when thou walkest by the way, and when thou liest down, and when thou risest up.
>
> —Deuteronomy 6:4–7

In the gospel of Mark, Jesus informed the religious leaders of His day about the importance of monotheism (one God).

> And Jesus answered him, The first of all the commandments is, Hear, O Israel; The Lord our God is one Lord: And thou shalt love the Lord thy God with all thy heart, and with all thy soul, and with all thy mind, and with all thy strength: this is the first commandment.
> —Mark 12:29–30

C=Cultic

This will represent witchcraft, false teachings, and other belief systems such as Buddhism, Islam, and Hinduism. This also covers doctrines like astrology, meditation, reincarnation, and other New Age doctrines.

> But there were false prophets also among the people, even as there shall be false teachers among you, who privily shall bring in damnable heresies, even denying the Lord that bought them, and bring upon themselves swift destruction.
> —2 Peter 2:1

H=Humanist values

Situation ethics teaches it's right to do wrong if it turns out for your benefit. Lying, stealing, cheating, etc., are acceptable if it's for the "right" reason.

> All the ways of a man are clean in his own eyes; but the Lord weigheth the spirits.
> —Proverbs 16:2

> There is a generation that are pure in their own eyes, and yet is not washed from their filthiness.
> —Proverbs 30:12

F=Fear

Fear can be good, like the fear of the Lord, or a fear of becoming pregnant, which keeps a girl from engaging in premarital activities, a young man that fears his parents enough not to drink. These are not the fears we are talking about. The fears we are talking about are fears generated by the devil to control people.

The Bible in 1 Timothy 1:7 tells us that fear can be generated by the supernatural.

> For God hath not given us the spirit of fear; but of power, and of love, and of a sound mind.

Many of the villains (and even the heroes) in today's cartoons are supernatural and extremely violent characters. Some cartoons have a minute by minute habit of violently killing characters and then often portray them return to life. This leaves our children with a skewed reality concerning the finality of death. Besides impacting young minds with an erroneous understanding of life, death and the supernatural, the violence in much of today's entertainment, cartoons in particular, leave children desensitized about the consequences of violent acts.

This kind of fear produces two different responses.

1. Fear may cause the person to be unable to sleep. It may lead them into a paranoid state, or feeling that they are being targeted. This could possibly lead to severe psychological problems.

2. They can enjoy the effects that the adrenaline produces, and become addicted to adrenaline. The danger with this is that the more we are willingly exposed to fear that produces adrenaline, the more our bodies become immune to its effects. Therefore, like any drug, you have to take more to produce the effects. An example would be the

two young men who killed those young people at Columbine High School. The fear that was going through those young men would have stopped the average person from doing such a horrible thing. But to them it became the ultimate adrenaline rush. Children today have been so exposed to fear that they have an incredible tolerance to it. What we as parents feared twenty years ago, children laugh at today. The reason why movies have to get more violent and concerts more outlandish is because of the desensitized state of this generation.

Don't get discouraged if the selection of programs your children can watch is very limited. The devil is setting the stage for the master deceiver known as the Antichrist. Just remember that before the Antichrist comes on the scene, the world will all be on the same page spiritually. However, there is a wealth of good programming available to build up your family in Christ, if you'll just take the time to seek it out and make the decision that no unclean thing shall enter your home. We praise the Lord for the variety of Christian programming (and even toys) available today through both Christian bookstores and retailers and through many different ministries.

Our prayer is that God will give you the strength to stand for what is right before the Lord. And we pray that your children will be like the three Hebrew boys in the book of Daniel who would not bow to the world's pressure, even if the devil wants to throw them in the fire.

The Rating System

V=Violence   M=Mythology   C=Cultic

H=Humanistic   F=Fear

Program	Rating
Aladdin	V C H
Angry Beavers	V H F
Back to Sherwood	V C H

Beast Wars	V C H
Casper	C H
Captain Planet	V M C H F
Digimon: Digital Monsters	V M C H F
Disney's Hercules	M C F
Dungeons and Dragons	V M C H F
Gargoyles	V M C F
Little Mermaid	M C H
Mummies Alive	V C
Mythic Warriors	V M C F
Power Rangers	V C H
Sailor Moon	V C
Smurfs	V C H
Tales from the Cryptkeeper	V C F
Tiny Toon Adventures	C H

This is in no way a complete list. There are currently over one hundred thirty different children's programs on television each day. This is just a sample of how our rating system works. It is our prayer that before your child is allowed to view these programs alone, you will take this system and the time to research the programs.

A great place to begin evaluating whether a particular program or activity is worthy of entrance into your home is to start with the rating guide we've offered and then ask the simple question, "Will the program in question produce the fruit of the spirit found in Galatians chapter five?"

> But the fruit of the Spirit is love, joy, peace, longsuffering, gentleness, goodness, faith, meekness, temperance: against such there is no law.
>
> —Galatians 5:22–23

Scripture points out that the opposite reflect acts which are destined for judgment.

Now the works of the flesh are manifest, which are these; adultery, fornication, uncleanness, lasciviousness, idolatry, witchcraft, hatred, variance, emulations, wrath, strife, seditions, heresies, envyings, murders, drunkenness, revellings, and such like: of the which I tell you before, as I have also told you in time past, that they which do such things shall not inherit the kingdom of God.

—Galatians 5:19–21

Adultery (sex with someone other than your spouse)
Fornication (sex outside of married)
Uncleanness (impure motives)
Lasciviousness (unbridled lust, without shame)
Idolatry (the worship of false gods)
Witchcraft (an abuser of drugs, sorcery, magical arts)
Hatred (revenge)
Variance (contention, strife)
Emulations (a form of uncontrollable jealousy)
Wrath (quick to anger)
Strife (self-seeking pursuit of power or office by unfair means)
Seditions (dissension, division)
Heresies (lies taught as Christian doctrine)
Envyings (desiring what others have, coveting)
Murders (the taking of innocent lives)
Drunkenness (consuming alcohol uncontrollably)
Revellings (to carouse . . . in modern terms, a "party animal")

Which Scriptures do the cartoons (and other programming) watched in your house represent? The blessings of verses twenty-two and twenty-three, or the curses of verses nineteen through twenty-one?

Chapter 14

Hollywood: "Spaced Out"— More Than Just Fantasy

In chapter eight we mentioned how Hollywood's movie machine had churned out an exorbitant number of movies and programs portraying UFOs, alien beings, and the supernatural. We want to reprise that theme here to spotlight how Hollywood's most influential names have produced films inundated with their own religious leanings. It is no coincidence that many of the top films and TV shows in history have worked in concert to strengthen the case for the existence of aliens and have simultaneously denigrated biblical beliefs. To illustrate this, we have selected three men whose works became household words worldwide: Gene Roddenberry of *Star Trek*, George Lucas of *Star Wars*, and Steven Spielberg of *E.T.: The Extraterrestrial*.

Star Trek—Gene Roddenberry

Gene Roddenberry was the creator of the wildly popular and groundbreaking TV series "Star Trek." As an atheist, Roddenberry's treatment of God was expectedly nonbiblical. Several "Star Trek" episodes included "god" characters, and though Roddenberry neither actually wrote nor produced any of these, they followed his original lead of being critical of alien religions, which are usually disguised earth faiths.

In the 1989 movie *Star Trek: The Final Frontier* (written and directed by William Shatner) the crew searches for God, only to discover that the god they had assumed was the creator is, in reality Satan, a self-grandiosing non-omniscient, cosmic freeloader. The conclusion to the plot of this, the fifth in the *Star Trek* movie series, points to mankind actually being god. That is exactly what humanism teaches—that there is no God, that you are your own master. From the original lie in the Garden of Eden (Genesis 3:5) to the self-enthroning of Antichrist in Jerusalem (2 Thessalonians 2:4), Satan's lie that man can be or is actually God continues. The rebellious lure that man is God was his downfall in the Garden and will be the keystone of his judgment at the Great White Throne.

A couple of notes about Roddenberry and "Star Trek": Gene Roddenberry was born in El Paso, Texas, in 1921 and became antireligious at an early age. As a youth, he attended a Baptist church where his mother taught Sunday school, but it was not until he was sixteen that he began to turn his back on Christianity.

> I remember complete astonishment because what they were talking about were things that were just crazy. It was communion time where you eat this wafer and you are eating the body of Christ and drinking His blood. My first impression was "Jesus Christ, this is a bunch of cannibals they've put me down among. . . ." I guess from that time it was clear to me that religion as largely nonsense, was largely magical, superstitious things.
>
> —Gene Roddenberry, from *Star Trek Creator*, by
> David Alexander, Roc, New York, 1994, pp 36- 37

From the above quote it is obvious that Roddenberry either never understood Christian doctrine, such as communion, or simply repeated his commentary on it in later life as a mantra to convince himself and others to ignore the existence of God. In 1986 he joined the American Humanist Association, and in 1991 was awarded the AHA Humanist Arts Award. Roddenberry passed away a short time later in October of 1991.

In fairness to William Shatner, we want to point out that though he was the original author of the script for *Star Trek: The Final Frontier*, it was one of his co-writers, producer Harve Bennett who introduced the story line which transformed God into Satan. It appears to us that though Shatner has been identified with New Age leanings in the past, the original script probably reflected a somewhat orthodox view of God and the devil. It appears that he became overpowered by studio politics and producer Harve Bennett, who rewrote the story line mid-production. Shatner stated:

> With Harve and the studio suits both worrying that my story, featuring appearances by both God and Satan, would more than likely offend a lot of moviegoers, Harve came up with the idea that perhaps we should alter the story and turn God and Satan into an evil alien pretending to be God for his own gain. This was a huge change, lightening the script considerably, and as I look at it now I can clearly see my acceptance of this most basic revision as my first mistake. I'd slowly but surely allowed my original story to become significantly diminished. God and the Devil were gone, replaced by a mere cosmic pretender to the throne, and much of the inherent dramatic tension that would have crackled between our main characters throughout the second half of our film was now similarly diluted.
>
> —Quoted from *scifimovies.about.com/movies/ scifimovies/gi/dynamic/offsite.htm?site= http://members.aol.com/Kirks1701A/index.htm*

Though Roddenberry publicly denounced the finished movie, with his anti-Christian bias he's certain to have privately approved of Bennett's scripting of God actually being Satan. As for Paramount Pictures believing that a story that portrayed both God and Satan was too controversial, we say, give us a break! Is it just us, or can anybody else gather the blatant anti-Christian bias that the studio showed in convoluting the biblical characters, no matter how unscriptural Shatner's rendition of them may have eventually become? How offensive is the thought of it somehow being controversial to script God vs. Satan? (No wonder so many view the words "Hollywood" and "atheism" as synonyms.) Perhaps they believed that the average sci-fi fan couldn't handle even a glimpse of basic biblical thought and that if they allowed the script to stand, it would somehow tarnish the humanistic history of "Star Trek." Most likely, it just rubbed the "studio suits" the wrong way due to their own anti-biblical vent.

Star Wars—George Lucas
Another of Hollywood's heavyweights is George Lucas, renowned producer and the creator of the *Star Wars* series. It is well documented that Lucas relies heavily on New Age philosophies and mysticism. The same are reflected throughout the series of *Star Wars* movies. In the 1970s it was no secret that Lucas used *Star Wars* as a vehicle to further his own (then) Buddhist leanings. Once telling *People* magazine that he had actually created *Star Wars* to reach America with a "good dose of Zen," an examination of the characters and script prove that he had indeed done so.

The "Force" Is Within You?
Obi-Wan (Ben) Kenobi, the heroic older Jedi Knight and mentor of Luke Skywalker, encourages his young student repeatedly to "use the force." Once, while teaching Luke the psy-

chic skills necessary to repel small flying robots with his light saber, Obi-Wan instructed, "Luke . . . Luke, use the force! The force is **within** you!" This is a model of Zen pantheism, the New Age belief that all beings have a god-force within them. This, of course, is only a counterfeit of the Holy Spirit of God who resides in us, does indeed lead us, and is a "force" within us after conversion to Christianity. Kenobi also lends support even from beyond the grave, necromantically communicating with Luke, reminding him of the force.

In the second *Star Wars* film, *The Empire Strikes Back* we are introduced to the character of "Yoda." Luke Skywalker, being led by a "spirit message" from the deceased Ben Kenobi, crash lands in a swamp on the mysterious planet Dagobah, and comes upon this small, strange creature who is to continue instructing him in the ways of "the force." Desiring to indoctrinate viewers with his spiritual beliefs through the film, Lucas grinds all action to a halt for over half an hour midfilm. During this time, Yoda thoroughly teaches the tenets of becoming a Jedi Master to Luke. Doctrinally, each time the film used the term "Jedi Master," one could easily insert "Zen Buddhist Master" instead. The swamp scenes climax with Yoda mystically using "the force" to not only levitate Luke's space craft out of the mire, but also employed telekinetic aportation to move it to dry ground! Both of these "mind over matter" exercises are well documented as occult practices. But neither has ever received so pointed an endorsement, to so many, in such a powerful medium as a motion picture of this caliber. The second movie reinforces the theme taught in the first: that "the force" resembles the yin and yang of Zen embodied in Skywalker and Vader. In other words, there is a little evil in all good and a little good in all evil. This is obviously *not* what the Bible teaches at all and if we don't have it to go on and judge and test *all things* that come our way, we are doomed to fall into Satan's quicksand.

In film three of the series, *Return of the Jedi* we are introduced to the hierarchy of those entrusted with "the force," an expansion on its powers and a mysterious planet named *Endor*, where the Empire has chosen to build a second, more ominous, "death star." One of the most dramatic scenes in this film comes after Yoda's death. Luke, angry, frustrated, and hurt, is crying out for answers. Obi-Wan Kenobi appears to him from the dead and consoles him saying, "Luke, you are going to find out that many of the truths we cling to depend greatly on our own point of view." Shortly thereafter, Luke asks Obi how to know right from wrong. Obi answers, "Luke, you will know right from wrong when you are at peace with yourself." These two statements are nothing less than blatant New Age relativism being poignantly and powerfully communicated by the "wise seer" via necromancy.

In 1999, after a twenty-two year lapse, Lucas released *The Phantom Menace*. The first in the *Star Wars* series (the original *Star Wars* movie was actually the fourth in Lucas' nine connected plots) takes us back to see the boyhood character that eventually becomes the sinister Darth Vader.

In an article in *Time*, (April 26, 1999) Lucas freely admits to interviewer Bill Moyer that he borrowed freely from many religious beliefs for the movie. Reviewer Rogier Bos correctly writes in his article "The Theology of Star Wars" (*www.nextwave.org/may99/starwars.htm*) that Lucas takes a very postmodern view of religion. Bos states:

> He sees religion as beneficial to human beings, even if what they believe is not actually true. To him the stories of the great religions are "myths" that are out of fashion, but whose themes are still very relevant. . . . Lucas explains very well a view of God and religion that I find everywhere I go. The understanding that God is everywhere like a force; the concept that this force that can be accessed through faith, and

the notion that we must break free from our rationalist mindset—all these are notions I hear all the time. . . . Lucas very clearly believes in God, although he has no idea what God is like. . . . What is also striking to me is that there is a strong influence of Eastern mysticism in this worldview. Lucas correctly calls it a Buddhist way of saying things. Thinking about contemporary culture, it is interesting to me that while the Judeo-Christian influence in culture is disappearing fast, the Buddhist or Eastern mystical worldview is in fact gaining ground rapidly.

How true this is, and Lucas was inspirational to those who in the 1970s began rushing toward the mystic East. Besides the musical groups the Beatles and the Beach Boys, Lucas may have introduced more Americans to Eastern philosophies and practices than any other person in our time.

In the *Time* interview, Moyer asks Lucas: "Is one religion as good as another?" Lucas answers:

I would say so. Religion is basically a container for faith. And faith in our culture, our world, and on a larger issue, the mystical level—which is God, what one might describe as a supernatural, or the things that we can't explain—is a very important part of what allows us to remain stable, remain balanced.

Moyers then states:

One explanation for the popularity of *Star Wars* when it appeared is that by the end of the 1970s, the hunger for spiritual experience was no longer being satisfied sufficiently by the traditional vessels of faith.

Lucas responds:

I put the Force into the movie in order to try to awaken a certain kind of spirituality in young people—more a belief in God than a belief in any particular religious system.

That he did. Throughout the article, Lucas refers to Buddha several times and the idea of all inclusionary religion, as if religion in and of itself is all humankind needs. Though Lucas seems to have slightly changed his religious views over the years, there can be no doubt that though he promotes the idea of "god," the "god" of George Lucas is not the one outlined by Scripture as the Creator of all things. Rather, it is an all–inclusive figure who can be found through any and all religions.

This is an intimate look at someone who is arguably one of the most powerful individuals in Hollywood history. If anyone thinks that story lines and scripts from Hollywood happen only by accident, they need to think again. To further illustrate this point, let's examine the naming of the character Yoda and the use of the title "Endor" for the Ewok planet in *Return of the Jedi*. They confirm the depth that Lucas went to in associating actual religious overtones.

Endor was a biblical location mentioned three times in the Old Testament. The most notable reference to Endor is the witch at Endor, whom King Saul sought out in 1 Samuel 28.

Yoda is certainly one of the most important characters in Lucas' entire *Star Wars* production. Though spelled differently, Yoda, the all-wise seer, the look of whom forty years ago would have caused nightmares but now is a child's plaything, seems to have been named from the Hebrew word *Yada*, which means "prognosticator" and "to know" or "to ascertain by seeing" (*Strong's*, #3045). How interesting, for this is exactly what Yoda does in the *Star Wars* story line.

We found nothing conclusive to indicate that Lucas is either Jewish by birth or raised in a Christian home. He says that at age ten he asked his mother why if there was but one God, were there so many religions. It appears she could not give him an answer and he has never sufficiently answered the question either. Perhaps this indicates why he has arrived at universalism as his religious worldview.

While recuperating from a serious auto accident, Lucas came up with "the force" by studying the writings of New Age intellectual mythologist Joseph Campbell. Campbell's books, *Myths to Live By*, *The Power of Myth*, and *The Masks of God*, are very visible in New Age circles (we found them through Castlebooks, publisher of *New Age Magazine*). Clearly, Campbell's view of God was ethereal and based in universalism also. Any affinity he had for Campbell's spiritual philosophies, coupled with his presumably aimless and unmentored spirituality as a boy, explains Lucas' view of religion and the identity of "god."

The world would question why Bible believers are so hard on universalist ideas. It is because if there is indeed another path to God, why did Jesus have to go through such a horrible death on the cross? Universalism is a direct affront to Christianity and Jesus' sacrifice for us. Without ever voicing it, universalism says, "God is a mean, cruel God who beckoned His own son to die a needless death."

We commend Lucas' awareness that our culture, young people in particular, are faced with a wide religious void and a gaping loss of values. However, merely filling that void with something is surely not the answer. Filling our spiritual voids with the *right* thing is the ultimate spiritual experience. Different from Gene Roddenberry's blatant coldness to spiritual things, George Lucas seems to be on a search for God. How nice it would be if we got credit for just believing there is a "god," but we do not. We realize that this does not sit well with the majority of the world outside the Christian faith. It is this line of thinking that causes the world to direct ire at those of us who believe the Scriptures—just as Jesus warned us would be the case. However, it cannot be helped. The truth *is* the truth and there *is* but one way to heaven. So Lucas, without the acceptance of the "God of all Gods" and "Lord of all Lords" is destined to the same fate as any atheist. Thankfully though, as long as he has breath, there is hope!

E.T.: The Extraterrestrial—Steven Spielberg

E.T. is perhaps the most famous creature to fly into your theater from space via Hollywood to date. Though certainly not sinister in comparison to many of the other sci-fi flicks of today, *E.T.: The Extraterrestrial* may have been far more damaging to young people and families. We know that to some it will sound as if we're trying to preach some sort of legalism, but that's simply not the case. Most of us can assess when something is blatantly evil, but our experience tells us that the more innocent or benign a TV show, cartoon, or movie appears, the more likely it is to slip under our critical parental judgment. If a movie carries a "G" or "PG" rating, yet indeed has occult, paranormal, or blasphemous content, it is often regarded as acceptable in the eyes of less discerning parents. Such was the case with *E.T.* The blatant God–mockery portrayed in this lighthearted movie is unmistakable.

Besides the obvious surreal fare that accompanies scripts built around beings from outer space, *E.T.* is perhaps more offensive to Jesus-loving Christians than the majority of violent and satanic films. The reason being that astute viewers will count more than thirty occasions in the movie where Steven Spielberg's story has E.T. paralleling the story of Jesus' life from the Bible. Though some have taken this to be a compliment to Christ, we do not. Here are just a few instances to illustrate our point.

- E.T. came from out of this world, indicated that he had to leave here, but promised to return someday. So did Jesus.
- E.T. pointed at his young friend Elliott and promised to live inside him always. Followers of Jesus have the same promise from the Lord.
- E.T. possessed the power to heal. Jesus healed.
- E.T. exhibited power over gravity and could travel about supernaturally (remember E.T. sitting on the handlebars of Elliott's bicycle as they soared through the air?). Jesus defied gravity.
- In a powerful scene, E.T. dies (supposedly from earth pollution) and then resurrects from the dead. Jesus died and rose again but to save man from sin—not from fluorocarbons! But true to the model, E.T. seemed to impart life through his dying and subsequent resurrection.
- In perhaps the most dynamic mockery in the movie, the creature ascends into the clouds with his followers watching and weeping. In the ascension, Jesus left this world as His followers stood in awe, watching Him go.
- One thing Jesus certainly didn't do was get fall-down drunk on Coors beer as E.T. did!

E.T.: The Extraterrestrial was nominated for nine Academy Awards, winning four. For over fifteen years, it was the **number one** most successful movie in Hollywood history. Let's remember that this movie was produced and directed by Steven Spielberg, one of America's most powerful New Age minds. This was **not** a promotion of Jesus Christ in any way. Instead, this was a "different christ" figure being heralded, one who came from space and who become a recognizable symbol in American life and around the world. Though the face of E.T. was modeled after the faces of poet Carl Sandburg and Albert Einstein, E.T.'s grotesque features should have scared moviegoers. Instead, the public fell in love with him.

Isn't it strange that it wasn't long ago that an image such as E.T.'s would have been a child's worst nightmare, causing fear and panic? Yet since the release and re-release of the movie, E.T. has become the *desired* dream of children: a friend; a playmate; a hero. This three-fingered, three-toed little beast (demonic manifestations are said to have three fingers and three toes) has become an irreplaceable icon in our culture.

While we do not believe there necessarily has ever been a covert conspiracy in place between Roddenberry, Lucas, Spielberg, or any of Hollywood's other writers, producers, or directors, there can be no doubt that Satan has used them widely and rewarded them greatly. We have not picked out obscure movies or TV programs. Two of these movies, *E.T.* and *Star Wars*, have at different times been the **number one** financial box office hit of all time, and "Star Trek" continues to spin off new TV series and movies more than thirty years after its inception. Those responsible have simply woven their belief systems into their work and the devil has promoted it in the furtherance of his kingdom. Regardless of how well produced or popular their end product may be, we believe that Christians need to be about the business of exposing the truth concerning these men and their work. They and others have surely provided a great service to Satan in preparing the mind of the culture concerning UFOs and supernatural beings.

Who are the "False Prophets"?
"Counterfeit Signs and Wonders" Come to Life
Scripture is replete with warnings about false prophets. Deuteronomy 13, 1 John 4, 2 Peter 2, and other passages, give us information about them. In Matthew 24, the famous "end times" chapter, Jesus powerfully outlines the work of false prophets, which is to produce great signs and wonders to

deceive many. When Antichrist comes, we know that he and his entourage will display a vast array of supernatural talents that will help convince the world to follow him. These signs and wonders will shock, stimulate, and awe the masses. So we shouldn't be surprised that the conditioning process, desensitizing and preparing the world for the Man of Sin and his reign of terror, is well under way.

In 2 Thessalonians 2:8–9 the apostle Paul brings this point home.

> And then shall that Wicked be revealed, whom the Lord shall consume with the spirit of his mouth, and shall destroy with the brightness of his coming: Even him, whose coming is after the working of Satan with all power and signs and lying wonders. . . .

Now at first glance it appears that Paul is only restating what Jesus has already proclaimed, but it is something different. Both Jesus and Paul are speaking about the signs connected to the Tribulation period and both are talking about signs that will destroy lives through deception. However, here in 2 Thessalonians, Paul expressly mentions these signs as "lying," whereas in Matthew 24 Jesus makes no such delineation. Paul also denotes that these lying signs take place around the time of Antichrist's "coming." What does this tell us? First, it appears that the signs are not the real miraculous wonders that Jesus describes in Matthew 24. Next, when you mention that someone is coming, it does not infer that they are actually present yet, but only that they are expected to arrive sometime soon. One version of the Bible notes here that the coming of the lawless one is displayed in all kinds of counterfeit miracles, signs, and wonders. The original Greek bears this out. Thus, when considering both Jesus' words in Matthew 24 and Paul's here in 2 Thessalonians, we see that there will be feigned or contrived signs as the Antichrist approaches, followed by *real* signs when he actually arrives.

With the advancements in technology we have today and with the skill and enormous financial resources at Hollywood's finger tips, we know of no more powerful display of *counterfeit, lying signs, and wonders* in history than those being constantly produced for consumption on the huge silver screen. There is no question that many of today's movies and TV shows are to a large extent made up of special effects—counterfeit wonders. Though completely incognizant of it, Hollywood is at least to some degree fulfilling this prophetic end-time passage of Scripture right before our very eyes!

When Jesus came, His people, the Jews, did not recognize Him. Instead of seeing Him as Messiah, they killed Him. In the same way, Satan wishes to blind the eyes of God's people today so that we won't understand the manner in which his *false messiah* is coming. We dare say that this is one of the most important things we've mentioned in this book. Our ability to wage Spiritual Warfare effectively hinges upon our understanding of the enemy's maneuvers. With all of the false cults and accompanying false prophets in the world today, can you think of any of them who have been able to accomplish Satan's work of preparing the world mindset for Antichrist more effectively than the false prophets he has working in Hollywood?

Chapter 15
The "Magick" of Harry Potter

The story of author J. K. Rowling's life is a classic rags-to-riches tale. She began writing the first Harry Potter book while living with her young daughter in a tiny flat in Edinburgh, Scotland. At the time, she was an unemployed teacher receiving government assistance and probably never dreamed of having the kind of success that's come her way via the Harry Potter book series thus far. After being published, *Harry Potter and the Philosopher's Stone* received rave reviews in England. The book became a literary sensation and was voted British Book Awards Children's Book of the Year and winner of the Smarties Prize. After being picked up in the United States by Scholastic Press, the title was changed to *Harry Potter and the Sorcerer's Stone*. It became an instant success worldwide.

Rowling has now published four books in the series. Besides *Sorcerer's Stone*, the series now includes, *Harry Potter and the Chamber of Secrets*, *Harry Potter and The Prisoner of Azkaban*, and the 734-page *Harry Potter and the Goblet of Fire*. The books are advertised for ages nine to twelve.

We were working on preparing this book the week that *Goblet of Fire* was released. Before the release, the Barnes &

Noble booksellers web site was akin to a monument for Harry Potter. A contest link on their web site advertised, "Can you divine the future?" and asked readers to click and then leave their ideas as to what the story line of the new book might be. When the book was released, it was already a *New York Times* best seller, just as its three predecessors had been, this time with an astonishing first run of 5.3 million books in English.

To attest to the popularity of Harry Potter, the day we sent this book to our publisher in September 2000, Harry Potter books ranked as four of the top five sellers at Amazon.com, the world's largest online retailer.

If you are thinking that the Harry Potter phenomenon is going to subside, we can assure you that it is not. In fact, it has doubtlessly inspired many other books of its kind (still to be published) to quench the thirst of young budding occultists lured by the Potter intrigue.

The bestselling Harry Potter series had already sold over thirty million copies in thirty-one languages before the release of *Goblets of Fire*. Additionally, Rowling has signed contracts to write a total of seven Potter novels, with each one becoming a film. *Harry Potter and the Sorcerer's Stone* is set for a November 2001 release by Warner Brothers. She has also warned that each book would be progressively darker. She wasn't kidding.

At the Potter's House

This is the description given on the OK UK Books web site for the first Harry Potter book, *Harry Potter and the Sorcerer's Stone*.

> Harry Potter is an ordinary boy who lives in a cupboard under the stairs at his aunt and uncle's house. Little does he know that his life is to change irrevocably when he is

rescued by an owl and taken to Hogwort's School of Wizardry and Witchcraft, learns about his parents' mysterious death, and comes face to face with the evil Voldemort in a deadly duel. . . .

Here is another description, this time from *Newsweek*.

Firmly in the eccentric tradition of the English children's story, Harry, like Peter Pan and Mary Poppins, can fly. Like Tolkien's Bilbo Baggins, he is surrounded by fantastical creatures. His boarding school is full of dotty profs and snobby brats, but it is also a world where owls deliver the mail and instead of chemistry and gym they study potions and transfiguration.

—Malcolm Jones, "Magician for Millions,"
Newsweek, August 13, 1999

Among the terrifying images in books two and three were: a disembodied voice repeatedly hissing "kill"; monstrous, flesh-eating spiders; children being attacked and paralyzed; and an apparently dead cat hung upside down by its tail (*USA Today*, June 15, 2000).

In book four of the series (*Goblet of Fire*) the evil character named "Wormtail" cuts up Harry's arm to extract blood in order to bring "Voldemort" (the most evil character) back to life. (This is an occult practice done to supposedly pass mystic power from one person to another during some occult rituals.) Rowling called Voldemort a "raging psychopath, devoid of the normal human responses to other people's suffering . . ." (*Entertainment Weekly*, #554, August 11, 2000). Also in the latest epic, Harry's parents, who have been killed, have to be extracted from Voldemort's magic wand. What kind of books are these and what inspires Rowling's work? We believe we know. She said, "It's important to remember that we all have magic inside us . . ." during an interview being taped for a "Scholastic Book Fair" video. And when asked in an August 2000 *Entertainment Weekly* interview by writer Jeff Jensen if she felt any sense of social responsibility (for the dark nature of the content of Harry Potter) Rowling answered, "I cannot write to please other people." She then goes on to mention that parents are coming to her saying their six-year-old "loved her book"! Perhaps a more important questions is, what kind of parents are these?

Is J. K. Rowling a real, practicing, bona fide witch? Our research turned up no overt statement she has made to make us believe so. However, when Ms. Rowling was asked about her favorite holiday, it was Halloween. We realize that many people who are *not* occultists might respond this way, but we figured her answer wasn't going to be Valentine's Day! What makes us explore this possibility further is just the occult accuracy of the texts. She has also intimated that some of the scenes in the books were fashioned out of real life experiences she's had. While from the materials and interviews we researched Rowling only named some railroad scenes portrayed in her writings as something actually from her childhood, it's not a huge leap to believe that the occult crux of the Harry Potter story could be from personal experience as well.

Whether Rowling herself is a witch or avid New Age dabbler, it is obvious that no one is really trying to veil the tie between the Harry Potter series and the occult, quite the opposite in fact. On the ABC.com web site there is a page dedicated to Harry Potter information. There, we found a link titled "Divination Class with Professor Susan Miller." The link led unsuspecting kids to famed astrologer Susan Miller's forecasting page.

While we are aware that much of the world praises Rowling's stories due to the supposed life lessons and ethical content taught in them, we more than question how a biblical

Christian could rationalize around the occult and increasingly more disturbing content in the Harry Potter series. Scripture demands that we have nothing to do with the deeds of darkness (Ephesians 5:11). This is not the story of good vs. evil. Once again, it is the story of white magic (or magick, as it is spelled in the occult) opposed to black.

Now we don't want to give the impression that Harry Potter is the only book series we are concerned with. There are many others. As troubled as many parents are over the content of children's books such as *Fortune Telling: Love, Magic, Dreams, Signs and Other Ways to Learn the Future*; *Wizard's Hall*; *Ella Enchanted*; *So You Want to Be A Wizard*; Edward Eager's *Half Magic*; and the *Alice* series by Phyllis Reynolds Naylor, the *Harry Potter* series eclipses every other book or series of its kind *ever* produced—in both popularity and in revenue. Clearly, *none* have come close to capturing hearts like Harry Potter has.

The Marketing of Harry

Beyond the books, the marketing of Harry Potter is just now coming into its own. We found a web site offering an assortment of kid's toys, such as capes, magic hats, wands, and fake tattoos, each one designed to emulate Harry Potter and each one based on occultism and magic. The advertisement of the items called them a "starter kit for future witches and warlocks." Another web site claims to provide everything you need for a magical Harry Potter birthday party. It says:

> If your child is one of the millions enchanted by J. K. Rowling's magical "Harry Potter" series, then Family.com's Harry Potter Wizard party is for you! Children can't get enough of boy wizard Harry Potter and his out-of-this-world adventures. They'll love the chance to play out their favorite characters and scenes with our Potter-themed party planner.

Party guests will feel like real Hogwarts students, enrolling in wizard's school, battling a Basilisk, practicing their Quidditch skills and even taking a Potions class. Their feet may not leave the ground, but their fun and imagination will soar at this spellbindingly fun party.

Just what you hoped your child would do: enroll in Hogwart Wizard School; battle a Basilisk (a legendary fourteenth century reptile with fatal breath and glance); practice Quidditch (a game Rowling invented for the Potter series which utilizes levitation by another name); and take a class on magic potions!

Interestingly, Harry Potter has an odd birthmark on his forehead in the shape of a lightning bolt. In a promotional campaign before the release of the third book, six hundred fifty thousand lightning bolt tattoos were distributed to bookstores worldwide. We know that some will consider it a stretch, however the lightning bolt has long been a symbol of power in the occult and Satanism. If Harry Potter was a heroic Christian boy and not a warlock, we'd just think it was odd. But knowing who he is and what he does, again we see it as no coincidence.

Watch for Harry to soon be on a computer screen near you as well. August 11, 2000, Electronic Arts Inc. (EA) announced it had signed a deal to develop Harry Potter into both video and computer games. We wonder how deep the occult inferences and violence will be in the finished products.

Hasbro Corp. has also secured the rights to make and distribute Harry Potter trading cards. This is the same company who carries the Pokémon line.

We surmise that as parents are concerned about freebee's associated with Pokémon, the Back Street Boys and other objectionable materials that come accompanying their child's

"Happy Meal" via the drive-thru window, just wait until the first Harry Potter movie is ready to hit theaters in 2001! We'll guarantee that you will *not* miss the marketing barrage to be displayed then.

Harry Comes to Class

Naturally, Scholastic is very happy with the results of Harry Potter. Any moral obligation they might have had in the past has disintegrated from the haul of cash Rowling's work has brought in. According to *Variety Magazine*'s Jill Goldsmith (July 19, 2000) the U.S. publisher saw net income soar thirty–nine percent to $51 million, and revenue rise twenty percent to $1.4 billion for the fiscal year ended in June. Revenue for children's book publishing and distribution rose thirty-one percent to $872 million, primarily due to Harry Potter sales.

Some educators and parents have touted the use of Harry Potter books in teaching children to read. However, it strikes us odd that with so many words that are simply Rowling's own invention, the vocabularies of children using Potter books to learn to read could be skewed at best.

Here is a sample of terms from Harry Potter.

Animagi
Azkaban
Daedalus
Erised
Gryffindor
Malfoy
Quidditch
Slytherin
Voldemort

J. K. Rowling's literary agent, Christopher Little, told *USA Today* on June 22, 2000, that the books are now being sold in over one hundred countries, with Russia and China coming soon. He said "Rowling's books are particularly popular in Japan, as well as in Scandinavia and other parts of Europe. Only in the USA has there been a hostile reaction. (Some parents think the books glamorize witchcraft.)" Well, that's not entirely true, but we're guessing that anyone throwing water on the Harry Potter phenomenon is probably a Bible believer.

Reuters wire service reported on July 27, 2000, that a New Zealand school (Auckland's Birkenhead Primary School) has banned teachers from reading extracts of the resoundingly successful Harry Potter book series aloud after a complaint about the books' references to wizardry and magic.

In 1998, CNN reported that an uproar ignited in the tiny town of Zeeland, Michigan, when a teacher read some of the Harry Potter books aloud in a school classroom.

> The controversy started when a few children told their parents about the scary story from school involving witches, goblins, and enchantment. That didn't go over well with some residents, who were troubled by the tales of violent, magical battles, of partially decapitated ghosts and the drinking of unicorn blood.
>
> —CNN, July 6, 2000

After complaints from Christian parents the Jacksonville, Florida, public library system ceased giving out what they called the "Hogwarts Certificate of Accomplishment" to young Harry Potter fans.

> The certificate, meant to encourage children to read, honored its recipient for completing a term at Hogwarts School of Witchcraft and Wizardry, the school young Harry attends.

The books feature Harry fighting against the forces of evil, aided by spells, flying brooms and magical instruments.
—Associated Press, September 13, 2000

Reuters reported (September 20, 2000) that after a heated debate between pro- and anti-Potter parents and board members, the Durham Regional School Board (near Toronto, Canada) dropped its previous requirement to have parents sign a note of consent which would allow their children to be taught from Harry Potter books in classrooms. The board decided to remove the restrictions citing that they didn't wish to see particular children excluded from some classroom activities. We spoke with a trustee on the Durham School Board about this issue and in so doing we were told that the issue was far from settled. School Board members and trustees, many of whom are Christians, are very unsettled about the direction this issue has taken there. These authors see examples like this as just another good reason to educate our children and grandchildren in a truly biblical Christian school rather than secular environments.

Cases such as these seem to be getting more frequent. Both of these authors have received calls and e-mails from concerned parents and even a school bus driver who is increasingly more troubled by what she sees on her bus concerning Potter books and the associated role playing. Perhaps most telling have been the e-mails Eric has received since mentioning Harry Potter in his online newsletter (at *www.ericbarger.com*). Though several have been from ministers in support of our position, those that need to be mentioned here were a series of notes from a parent in Alberta, Canada, who alerted us that Potter books were being used in a *Christian* school there. Also, Eric received over a half dozen letters from teachers *defending* the use of Harry Potter. One of these included the following statements.

South Carolina schools challenged the Harry Potter books because, "the books have a serious tone of death, hate, lack of respect, and sheer evil." In the Frankfort, Illinois, School District, the Harry Potter books were challenged but retained. Parents were concerned that the books contained lying and smart-aleck retorts to adults.

Have you been in the streets lately, especially in poor areas of towns and cities? They have a serious tone of death, hate, lack of respect, and sheer evil. Should we ban those areas, or let the children read Harry Potter books so they can see how a kid with a bad attitude changed his attitude, changed his circumstances, and developed respect for those elders who respected him? . . .

Harry Potter books have an uplifting theme . . .

. . . should [we] ban most of the fairy tales and folktales and legends from other cultures that fill up much of the school and public libraries? Many of those folk tales have demons and witches and fairies and gremlins, trolls, talking animals, etc, where good triumphs over evil. How far are we going to go in banning books that have an uplifting, good over evil theme?

How can good triumph over evil, if there is no evil in the story and plot? If we ban all books with evil in them, how are we going to have our children read "make-believe" books that use analogy to teach a lesson or get an idea across?

This public school teacher, from Norman, Oklahoma, is a member of a good Bible-believing church. Without being overly critical of her, we want to point out that she has crossed the line into relativism, but more than that, in her defense of

Harry Potter she appears to have a blurred vision of what God expects of His children. The standard argument we have both heard school teachers give when defending New Age philosophies and practices in the classroom is, "Well, it works." Our rebuttal to this is simple. Just because something works, doesn't make it *right*! To the Christian, the "end" can never justify the "means," even if the outcome is positive. This teacher is right on one count however. We do face a world laced with folklore and fairy tales—each of which utilize white vs. black magick. (Keep in mind that white witchcraft vs. black is a joke among occultists.) The biblical truth is that these stories—no matter how accepted they are in our culture—present an anti-biblical view of evil and good. Though they may warm our hearts and touch the nostalgia buttons in our memories, they are, in reality, works of the devil. And concerning the case at hand, there must be an effective way of teaching children without glorifying a warlock named Harry Potter. As one pastor commented, "Allowing our children to read Harry Potter books (just because 'everybody else is') is allowing them to read nothing more than spiritual pornography." Have we forgotten our standards as believers? Perhaps our refusal to stand against the likes of Harry Potter and instead compromise with it is the worst part about all of this. The Bible says that Satan himself is transformed into an angel of light, and that his ministers will appear to be righteous (2 Corinthians 11:14–15). How far we have slipped from God's holy standard of spiritual discernment when there is even a hint of discussion favoring the likes of Harry Potter among believers.

Harry Potter's Religion

Witches have good reason to be excited about Harry Potter. The book series is giving the "craft" a huge boost. No wonder that when interviewed by *USA Today*, a warlock endorsed

Harry Potter and bubbled with excitement at the series' wide acceptance by the mainstream.

> He's a charmer, that Harry Potter. The adolescent hero of
> J. K. Rowling's series rides a broom, owns an invisibility
> cloak and magic wand, and has cast a spell over young
> readers the world over. He has modern-day witches en-
> chanted too. "For once, the witches aren't ugly old hags,"
> said Michael Darnell, 39, a computer programmer from
> Winnipeg, Canada, who has been a practicing witch for
> over twenty-five years. "For once they're the protagonists
> rather than the villains."
>
> —*USA Today*, May 30, 2000

In an interesting side note, the Dallas (Texas) City Council inadvertently invited a Wiccan minister from the Covenant of the Goddess Church to pray the invocation over their September 27, 2000, meeting. A hubbub erupted when the invitation was suddenly pulled. It seems that word got out and Christian radio stations in the Metroplex area began alerting listeners, bringing pressure to bear on the councilmen and mayor. Though an opening prayer offered by clergy is the normal course for the council to take, when they realized just who it was that was coming to "pray," they thought better of the invite.

When a local TV reporter asked Mayor Ron Kirk if he was worried about having spells cast on the council, the city, or himself, he answered no. Though Wiccan pickets lined the streets protesting the absence of occultist "Reverend" Bryan Lankford's invocation before the council, Kirk said he had read the four Harry Potter books and knew exactly what to do concerning spells and incantations!

We can assure you that we certainly sleep better here in Texas knowing that the mayor of Dallas has learned all about

"white" witchcraft from J. K. Rowling's boy-wizard! How sad
that the mayor's answer wasn't framed by Scripture pointing
to the cross of Christ as his protection. By the way, amid cries
of "bigotry" and "intolerance" from freethinking Texans, the
Wiccan priest was invited back the following week and did
indeed invoke a "blessing" at the opening of the council's session.

The Separation of Christianity and State, NOT State and Religion

The debate about whether Harry Potter books should be allowed in a school classroom setting ought to be a no-brainer
for the Christian—and the legal profession as well. Harry Potter is a clear endorsement of a recognized religion. When
teachers read, teach from, or use the Harry Potter series in
the public classroom setting, what we have is an obvious bias
favoring and even encouraging witchcraft. Would they dare
give the Bible equal time?

Each year, Halloween—witchcraft's most celebrated day—
is recognized at virtually every public school in our nation,
while Christmas has become a banned word on campus. It is
the same with Harry Potter. We doubt if the American Civil
Liberties Union (ACLU) will step in and help the concerned
folks in Zeeland, Michigan, and others. (For the most part,
"ACLU" seems to stand for "Antichrist Liberties Union," doesn't
it?)

It is obvious that we do not have a separation of state and
religion in America. In the United States, anti-Christian big-
ots hide behind what they *claim* the Constitution states, even
though there is no such separation called for in the docu-
ment. *What is being enforced all around us is a separation of
state and Christianity!* This is exactly the attitude that will
prevail when Antichrist comes.

What is troubling is that many who claim to be believers

view anyone making a stand against Harry Potter, Halloween, witchcraft itself, or any other work of the enemy as "radical" or "fanatic." Biblically however, how can we expect to enjoy the presence of God, His joy, and His protection in our homes when our kids are beholding a fictitious wizard as a hero and going trick-or-treating on October 31?

We were interested but dismayed by an online poll taken at the popular Ibelieve.com web site about Harry Potter. The question was asked, "Are you a fan of the Harry Potter series?" Out of over five hundred Christians responding, forty percent said "yes," seven percent said "no," and fifty-three percent were "undecided." Along these same lines in another survey, out of over eighteen hundred Christians polled, only fifty-two percent thought Christians should not go trick-or-treating. These two surveys further prove to illustrate the ignorance, confusion, and perhaps the rebellion against God's Word on issues like sorcery and the occult.

On Eric's ministry web site at *www.ericbarger.com* we asked the question, "Do you favor or oppose the Harry Potter book series?" The response was larger than any other poll ever taken on the site. Over sixty-four percent of the respondents answered that they opposed Harry Potter, but thirty-one percent said they favored the book series, with only about four percent marking "don't know" for their answer. It appears that if Eric's readership (markedly conservative) are close ideologically to that of Ibelieve.com's then the "undecided's" are thinning out with many readers coming down in favor of Harry.

Proving this, here are a few of the responses we got to our poll.

I have read all 4 books and enjoyed them. I have no qualms with my kids (8, 10, 12) reading them. Great use of imagination and good over evil.

> What is wrong w/the harry potter books? Like OMG they are gonna make kids wanna be witchs (sic)...OH NO!!!!! AHH!! stupid ppl.
> Have you ever read C. S. Lewis' Chronicle of Narnia series?!?!

> Imagination is a gift of God. . . . Please get off the soapbox and deal with more relative issues that we as Christians have been called to address!

We presume this writer meant to say "more relevant." If so, we'd like to know what more relevant issues Christians are called to address? The occult is addressed adamantly in the Bible and is certainly a relevant issue in our day. Millions are deceived and in the process of losing their souls because of satanic deceptions like Harry Potter. What's the problem? Why are we receiving opposition from inside the church? The answer is simply this: lack of willingness to be obedient to God's Word.

These authors have long been aware of this lack of understanding and/or willingness by some in the church to follow what is a clear-cut biblical standard concerning Satan's works. Most disturbing was another poll by Ibelieve.com which asked its readers, "Do you hold a leadership role within your church? Fifty-four percent answered, "yes." We assume many of the same people took part in each poll.

Adding to the confusion surrounding the Christian position concerning Harry Potter has been the endorsement of Potter books by some in positions of prominence in Christian circles today. Both *Christianity Today* and *Lutheran* magazines have given thumbs up to Harry. So has noted evangelical Chuck Colson. Is it through ignorance that those claiming to be Bible-believers have expressed positive views about Rowling's books? Certainly liberalism is continuing to encroach upon even the best of churches and denominations. But we perceive that many who view Harry Potter in an acceptable light may be doing so in a vain effort to somehow show the world that Christians aren't really too radical in their views after all. Like it or not though, Scripture presents the case that we *must* be removed from such things as witchcraft and sorcery—no matter what the world thinks of us. In the quest for inclusion there are some around us—some who are Christian leaders—who have no taste for taking hard stands. How tragic that by standing against nothing, eventually people will fall for anything! Perhaps we should examine that it is precisely this—our failure to address evil for what it is—that has allowed Satan to march into homes and hearts and set up camp.

As for those who somehow equate Harry Potter to the writings of C. S. Lewis or J. R. R. Tolkien, we submit that in these perilous times, with witchcraft rising to unparalleled peaks, that those wishing to truly guide their children toward the cross of Christ might well think twice before putting Tolkien or Lewis into their young hands. Would Lewis have written the way he did decades ago if he could have seen the occult explosion around us today? In times past allegories and even fantasy were sometimes helpful in presenting the Christian message. However, that was before animation technology gave rise to every sort of fantasy-world imaginable in such graphic detail and realism. Even though to some, Lewis showed sympathy toward paganism, if he was indeed the legendary apologist for Christianity that many make him out to have been, we think he would have used a different approach. (See *Surprised by Joy* and *Pilgrim's Regress* by C. S. Lewis. Also see "The Bewitching Charms of Neopaganism: Surprised by Lewis" by Loren Wilkinson, *Christianity Today*, November 15, 1999, Vol. 43, No. 13, Page 54.)

Potter defenders often try and parallel Harry with Lewis'

hero in the *Lion, the Witch and the Wardrobe* as well. Though we Christians know that Lewis' hero is a type of Christ, can one seriously insert Harry Potter—a warlock—into the same role just because he uses his magic for less ominous outcomes than his adversary does? Potter is a wizard utilizing satanic powers to accomplish his agenda. How can this be defended as even remotely acceptable by Bible believing Christians?

Let it be said once more—this should be a "no-brainer" for the Bible believer. How much clearer does Isaiah 5:20-21 need to be?

In making our case against allowing Harry Potter books and related merchandise to have a place in our homes and lives, we are not suggesting that parents should attempt to shield children from all knowledge that witchcraft, sorcery, and the occult actually exist. That would be fruitless in society today. The approach we support is to educate them, first in the immutable truth of Scripture and then in that context, to explain what the world around us believes and why. To be ignorant of Satan's devices goes directly contrary to the Bible, and while there certainly are practices and events that we should not share with our kids until a suitable age, we as parents and grandparents need to hone and develop communication with them that is limitless within the guidelines of Christian values.

The publishing industry rarely sees a phenomenon like Harry Potter. And there seem to be few detractors speaking their minds (and Bibles) as we are. A poll at CNN.com recorded almost nineteen hundred votes asking if Harry Potter was a bad influence on children. A landslide of ninety-five percent said "no." The results were not surprising considering the desensitization and ignorance about the occult by the general population. We know that our discussion on Harry Potter won't make us any friends among the millions of parents who have bought into the Harry Potter excitement. However, with all accolades from a spiritually blinded world aside, Harry Potter is a tremendous advertisement and endorsement for the occult. As much as these two authors have researched, ministered about, and discussed the role of the entertainment media and its effects on kids and families, we believe that the Harry Potter book series is perhaps one of the most potent tools to ever impact children's lives for Satan.

Chapter 16
The Weird World of Pokémon

While understanding the disturbing nature of Harry Potter may seem simple, quite the opposite is true with Pokémon. The Pokémon phenomenon, created several years ago in Japan, sprang from the popular Nintendo hand-held Game Boy video game and progressed to a 1998 TV cartoon series here in the United States. The marketing of Pokémon logo items includes just about any item of apparel imaginable, a vast set of trading game cards, toys, and now includes two hit movies and a traveling road show. Kellogg's, Kraft Foods, and Burger King are just a few of the outlets for Pokémon items. Hasbro paid $325 million for the rights to market the toys, and this year Pokémon receipts are expected to top a staggering **$7 billion** worldwide. Toy industry analyst Sean McGowan told *Newsweek* magazine (November 15, 1999), "In the history of the toy industry, there has never been a hit so global, so multimedia, so rapid, so long-lasting as Pokémon." Attesting to its popularity, we found more information on the Internet concerning Pokémon than one could ever care to read. From our research, one thing is evident. The trading cards and associated games are indeed the Pokémon centerpiece and mainstay.

For those who don't know about the Pokémon craze, it has grown to fanatical proportions. One example of this happened just before the release of the first Pokémon movie in November 1999. A Los Angeles radio station announced a phone-in contest to win tickets for the premiere of the movie. Suddenly the Warner Brothers switchboard was jammed, receiving seventy thousand calls *a minute!* The casual observer may think this is just another cute plaything like "Furby" was, or something to interest collectors like "Beanie Babies." However, it is far from innocent. Pokémon actually means "pocket monster" in Japanese. This is the essence of the entire Pokémon genre. It is based on a series of monsters aimed at children (primarily boys) ages four and up, packaged in just about every media form.

So what is the attraction? Why are these movies and the TV cartoon so tremendously popular? The animation is second rate, the characters have no heroic stature, and the movies are dreadfully produced. Pokémon has definitely produced lots of money from not much product. The movies and cartoons blur the senses and thinking with an extremely violent message, but no decipherable plot and very flat imagery. The movies and cartoons do one important thing—sell the products; in particular the trading cards and games. However, Pokémon is selling something else entirely.

The attraction to kids is the interaction they experience with the cards and games, but tragically, it is virtually all negative. The game teaches that Pokémon gives power to whoever carries them. The monsters use poison, electricity, fire, and psychic power to destroy other monsters. From the original Game Boys, to the trading cards, to the movies, the underlying theme behind Pokémon is merciless, violent domination and manipulation of others via occult powers.

When the movie *Pokémon 2000* was released, children were given the "Ancient Mew Card" at theaters. This card is riddled with mystic Egyptian, superstitious, and occult signs, but this is only the surface of Pokémon. The two animated movies, released in 1999 and 2000, portrayed primarily violence as different Pokémon characters interact to overcome one another by hitting, slapping, throwing, kicking, or casting spells. *Preview Family Movie and TV Review* said:

> . . . the constant violence and the associated violent games pose a serious concern about the Pokémon craze along with its apparent promotion of occultic-like phenomenon in associated games.

Film critic, Ann Hornaday, writing for *The Sun Spot* online service, November 10, 1999, said of the first movie release:

> Pokémon comes straight from the Short Attention Span school of the cinema. . . . This movie seems chiefly to be an excuse to sell even more trading cards, those elusive billets that have turned a generation of youngsters into thieves, mercenaries, and compulsive gamblers.

She isn't kidding.

Pokémon to the Poky

Numerous reports cite Pokémon as the culprit for what one writer described as a "kiddy crime wave." Here are a few examples:

The November 22, 1999, issue of *Time* magazine reported that a six-year-old logged on to a Pokémon web site and printed counterfeit copies of the cards to trade with gullible schoolmates.

Many schools have banned the cards from classrooms and some others from the campus altogether. The November 22, 1999, *Time* also reported:

When children bring the Pokémon cards into the lunch-room, they often spend time looking at the cards instead of eating lunch. . . . Children overly anxious to please their peers are also at greater risk for addictive behavior.

Malcolm Jones wrote in *Newsweek* (November 15, 1999) that one reason for the ban on Pokémon cards was that kids were actually stealing the cards from each other. They would be so caught up in the trading, after recess it would continue in the classroom where teachers were having to referee.

The article quoted that "cards cause the fights and tears when a trade goes bad. Hard-to-find cards command any-where from $100 to $400 on the Pokémon black market."

According to an ABC News wire report (December 30, 1999) a couple of grandparents were upset with language used by a toy Pokémon character.

A Christmas gift one couple had given their grandchildren has them in an uproar. The couple says the **Pokémon** toy they purchased at a local K-Mart spews obscenities. The talking Pikachu has gone from saying his name to saying a profane phrase. K-Mart officials say they will bring the matter to the attention of the Hasbro Corporation, the man-ufacturer of the toy. The couple plans to contact area mer-chants citing the foulmouthed Pikachu is inappropriate for kids.

But the damage Pokémon is inflicting on young lives goes far beyond simple childhood mischief or a toy incorrectly pro-grammed by a smart-alek factory employee. Again, the afore-mentioned issue of *Time* recorded that just a week previous to their publication date, a nine-year-old boy on New York's Long Island stabbed an older schoolmate in a dispute over cards.

The Associated Press carried an article entitled "Pokémon Creates Crime Wave" by Meki Cox on December 10,1999. Cox reported that in the first week of December, four Philadelphia children from one middle school were arrested for attacking other students to steal Pokémon cards and that a fourteen–year–old student in Quebec was recently stabbed during a fight over the cards. Another incident reported that week was the arrest of a North Carolina man who was charged with assault for allegedly punching a Burger King cashier after he did not get a Pokémon toy with his meal! Associated Press continued that during that same week at Philadelphia's Wilson Middle School, two boys punched and threw a trash can at an eleven-year-old boy in a bathroom. The attackers ran off with two Pokémon cards and seventy-five cents. They were charged with robbery and suspended for five days.

Tony Ward's ten-year-old son and his friend were robbed of sixty dollars worth of cards one Sunday in Philadelphia. He said he wishes his son wouldn't trade cards anymore. "But he insists on having them," Ward said. "Hopefully he has learned his lesson and won't carry around as many cards anymore. I tell him when he goes out he has to be more street smart now."

These authors question just why a ten-year-old is allowed to make up the rules he lives by anyway. And more so, is it obvious why we are concerned with the Pokémon craze? It is violence and greed, begetting the same, let alone the mystic-occult connection.

Pokémon Is Not a Slow, Harmless Jamaican!

Here are some things to consider before you write Pokémon off as just a "harmless fad."

The creator and distributor of the trading cards is a company called "Wizards of the Coast." These are the same people who brought you **Dungeons and Dragons**, **Advanced Dun-**

geons and Dragons, and **Magic: The Gathering**, just to name a few. **Magic: The Gathering**, for example, features spirits rising up from grave tops. Any child with access to the Internet who is looking for Pokémon cards can easily log on to the "Wizards of the Coast" web site and find information meant to entice Pokémon fans to explore more blatantly occultic games. The "Wizards of the Coast" web site advertises its wares as follows:

> **Dragon** *Magazine* is the ultimate resource for TSR role playing games, especially the **AD&D** game. Each issue is filled with information you can take straight to the gaming table, including resources like new character races, classes, kits, proficiencies, magical items, spells, monsters, and plenty more. **Dragon** *Magazine* is the authority on all things role-playing. Expand your knowledge of the games you play with the latest spells, magical items, kits and inside information found only in **Dragon** *Magazine*.

It is important to understand that Pokémon is a prime bait Satan is using to lure our children into the occult. **Dungeons and Dragons** was not a fad. It was only the first fantasy role playing (FRP) game that many of us became aware of. It has introduced perhaps millions of people to a dark, occult world.

Here, the "Wizards of the Coast" web site instructs Pokémon players about a part of the game called "Psychic Assault."

> There are a couple of things you will need to look out for when making and playing Psychic Assault. It might be hard to construct the deck if you have access to a very limited number of cards; there are a fair number of rare cards and holograms in the deck. When playing the deck, be careful against Psychic Pokémon, as all your Pokémon are weak

against Psychic. The up side here is that you have Psychic Pokémon as well in the deck, so an opponent who uses a lot of Psychic Pokémon will face the same difficulties as you.

Some of the cards your children will need in order to win are:

Mewtwo (handed out to moviegoers entering the *Pokémon 2000* movie.)
Abra
Kadabra
Alakazam

After reading about these cards on the "Wizards of the Coast" web site, we went to web sites operated by bona fide witches to illustrate what these words meant. This is what we found.

Abracadabra is a mystical word used to magically invoke benevolent spirits for protection against disease. This magical formula may be related to the word *abraxas* (if this word sounds familiar to you, the group "Santana" had an album by that same name years ago). This was found inscribed on many amulets during the last years of the Roman Empire and is thought to have originated with the Gnostics. In any case, *abracadabra* is just as effective as *abraxas* or *hocus–pocus*. According to Pokémon play rules, Alakazam is the evolution of Abra and Kadabra. These words were used in occult rituals well before Disney thought they would be cute to use.

As we've mentioned, witches invoke the five forces of earth, wind, fire, water, and spirits. (Refer to the chapter on witches for more information). These same elements are part of Pokémon as well. If your child plays Pokémon, knowing that witchcraft and psychic power go against the Word of God, what will they believe in later in life? It is spiritually confusing to say on one hand that God's Word is supreme and then allow our kids to possess occult playthings. Plus, it is spiritually damaging to allow these influences a place in our lives and homes. More than just damaging however, it is perilous as we open our lives up willingly to Satan's attacks and activities. As Christians, we have the Holy Spirit. Shouldn't our kids be versed in His workings, instead of Pokémon's?

If the possibility of allowing your child to play with and become emotionally and spiritually attached to occult items isn't convincing enough, think about this. Consider the friends your child could acquire from this game. This type of fantasy role-playing has the potential of attracting the worst friends imaginable for your kids. If your child goes to a public school, they now have a common denominator with those children that are not Christians. The neighbor's child, who always thought your child was a good Christian, will want them to go to gaming rooms to trade these cards.

Besides all the associated problems of cheating, greed, and violence associated with Pokémon, it creates and nourishes an environment for addictive patterns in children. Compulsive behavior is blamed on every problem we have in our society. Both of us have had alcoholics in our families. Both David and Eric were drug addicts, Eric for fourteen years and David was arrested for drugs and was sent to reform school. We understand addiction. These obsessive patterns are easily acquired. Years ago both of us started to collect baseball cards. That in itself is not bad. But David found himself looking for card shops in every town. He would spend hours at home sorting them instead of spending time with his family. It became an obsession to him so he stopped it. Pokémon has that same attraction. The idea that you can strike it rich by finding the rare cards is appealing in the natural. So children and adults are now spending their lunch money, allowances, and paychecks to seek the jackpot. Some of these cards are selling on shopping networks for hundreds of dollars. If you see your eight-year-old child begging, pleading, willing to do anything for Pokémon, don't be surprised when they will do anything for drugs, alcohol, cigarettes, or sex when they are sixteen. It can create an appetite for those things condemned in the Word of God.

All that needs to be said about Pokémon is that it is distributed by "Wizards of the Coast" and that the entire Pokémon power structure is based around psychic characters which represent divination and the case should be closed. Why do we need to give twenty-five reasons? With just the evidence we have presented, to play the games, let alone support the Pokémon phenomenon in general, one has to ignore biblical understanding.

We recognize we are dealing with issues of emotional attachment and financial addiction here. We know our words are not going to be popular with many young people and also with parents unwilling to admit they were wrong or uninformed by allowing Pokémon to gain a foothold in the homes. But this is an issue of obedience to the Lord—for us and for you, the reader. We realize that we are swimming against the tide of opinion *even in Christian circles* on this one, but that's not a new sensation for either of us.

Christian Confusion

One would think that from what we have already stated concerning Pokémon, there would be no controversy about the subject within the Christian community. However, that is not the case. As with some other cultural issues, a blasé, *laissez faire* attitude is emanating tragically from parents concerning Pokémon. Trying to discuss the occult and violent nature of Pokémon with some gets little more than a roll of the eyes or a chuckle in response.

Similar to the poll we cited from the Ibelieve.com web site concerning Harry Potter, some of the entries in the Ibelieve.com discussion board concerning Pokémon disturbed us as well. We remind you that although the entries and content of this web site appear to be decidedly conservative and biblical in orientation, however concerning Pokémon and Harry Potter some were exactly the opposite.

Here are a few sample responses from the Ibelieve.com discussion board on Pokémon.

> My wife and I have treated the card game as a tool. My son (who has the interest) has through playing, improved his reading and his math skills, and using the card guides, has worked on his money handling and haggling skills. None of our children really care for the toys (BK or otherwise), though the gold-plated cards are kinda cool. Most of the schools have banned trading during school hours, so most of the exchanges and games take place on the bus and at home. I sometimes play with him, using the deck to encourage critical thinking and strategy.

We question why in the world would a Christian parent see the need to use the violent and mystic nature of Pokémon to teach his child to read, reason, and "haggle," to use the writer's term? Why not use the Bible instead?

Another entry said:

> . . . like any other FANTASY game, it is what you make of it. I played D&D for years, as did the Pastor of my Church. He was one of the best Gamemasters. "Chronicles of Narnia" is fantasy, yet no one seems to argue its benefit.
>
> I don't know much about the cartoon, my kids rarely watch it. From the few episodes I have seen, the team that treats their Pokémon with Love and Respect, is the team

that wins, even if it isn't always a victory in battle.

As far as the card game. It is a strategy game. The Pokémon provide the weapons and through critical thinking the players must decide the best way to protect themselves and their Pokémon. They don't even use the term kill or destroy. They use remove from play, stun, knock out, etc. But this is just a FANTASY.

Eric wrote the writer of this entry the following response.

It would appear that you are caught in the trap of trying to define art with the framework of moral relativism. The church in our day is anemic and weak because we cannot seem to discern what is right from what is wrong. That is the crux of New Age thought.

It is not critical thinking to cite examples of history to make one's point . . . not, if we wish to walk in God's favor. It is intellectually liberalized thinking such as this that has slowly torn away at the authority of Scripture, turning it and God into what we want them to be . . . instead of us conforming to the Word and becoming what God wants us to be.

I believe your endearment to FRPs has blinded you to realize that occult involvement at any level is an open door for Satan's work. Whoever your pastor is, he needs to repent of occult-based FRPs, and my friend, so do you. I sure wouldn't want to sit under his teaching knowing that he's been influenced by D&D, and is not regretful and repentant of it.

Eric Barger
Take A Stand! Ministries
www.ericbarger.com

Then we read this response to the Pokémon question.

First all my kids are grown but I do have a grandson. I trust the Holy Spirit and also the Word of God and if it doesn't lift up the name of God, don't mess with it under any circumstances, no exceptions. Stand your ground as a parent and don't give in to pressure, whether from kids or other adults. God is calling His children back to Holiness and Righteousness. I am not ashamed of God's Word or His standards and I know he won't be ashamed of me. It isn't easy to do but the rewards are great. Try it.

Holiness? Righteousness? Is this lady old-fashioned? No, she's *God-fashioned*! We live in a world that cares only about self. That attitude is all too often prevalent within the church to-day as well. What a breath of fresh air—holy fresh air—to read that others still believe in God's Word as a standard, regardless of what society's lack of understanding and standards may be. This writer said, "It isn't easy to do, but the rewards are great." We say, **"Amen"**!

Perhaps the most telling entry of all was this:

I am confused. What is it about Pokémon that make them so bad? I am not being sarcastic. I really don't understand the big deal about a card stock with pictures of goofy animals.

These discussion board entries were some of the determining factors, which led us to give the issue of Pokémon the prominence we have in this book. Pokémon is just the kind of inroad that Satan desires with our kids. One entry in the Ibelieve.com discussion board said that Pokémon is just a fad. While that may be true, if we allow this to go unchecked, undiscussed, and misunderstood, Satan is sure to elevate the stakes with his next advance into our children's lives. We appeal to children, teens, and parents to consider this. Pokémon did not become a phenomenon because of great animation or because it is so original. It is because of peer pressure to participate and because Pokémon offers opportunity to create personal power, which for centuries has led millions down hell's path to violence, crime, addictions, and the occult.

The Bible tells us that we are a different people, set apart for God, and we have a higher calling. God offers His people the power of the Holy Spirit and all of the self-worth we'll ever be in need of. Pokémon offers only the counterfeit and does nothing to enhance our children's spiritual walk with God. Rather, it only detracts from it. Instead of collecting Pokémon items, shouldn't we be collecting the knowledge of God and tapping into His unending power, strength, and blessings?

Chapter 17

Halloween: This Trick Is No Treat!

In 1999, we released a pamphlet that outlined our concerns about Halloween. We've reprinted it here in its entirety.

When we were kids growing up, we always looked forward to Halloween. We knew nothing about how it began, or what the meanings were behind it. All we knew was that we could get dressed up funny and go through the neighborhood and people would give us candy.

The information you are about to receive is to help you understand the seriousness of Halloween. It is not to spoil your fun, but to ask the question: Should we, as Christians, join in a festival whose history and practices are for the dead? Today, with Halloween being a billion dollar business second only to Christmas in retailing, few understand the true nature and historic foundations of this occult celebration.

Origin of Halloween

The word "Halloween" actually has its origins in the Catholic Church. It comes from the words "All Hallows Eve," "All Hallows Day," or "All Saints Day." This day was set aside to honor saints. The holiday was founded to try and divert attention away from the pagan practices taking place on this day each October. Though perhaps well intentioned, trying to "Christianize" pagan practices can never be pleasing to God, and Halloween may be the most vivid example of this. Some believe Irish immigrants fleeing the potato famine may have brought its origins to America in the 1840s.

In occult and witchcraft circles, October 31 represents a day of worship called Samhain (pronounced *sow-en*). This is the Celtic New Year. History tells us that the Celtic people were worshipers of earth gods, woodland spirits, and sun deities. One legend explains that on Samhain the spirits of all those who had died throughout the year would come back in search of living bodies to possess for the next year. It was believed to be their only hope for entering the afterlife. It was also the day that the living were to communicate with the dead. This practice is called necromancy.

Deuteronomy 18:11 tells us that God considers this practice evil. We see examples of necromancy portrayed in movies like *The Sixth Sense, Lion King*, and *Ghost*, to name a few. Regardless of where or how the ritual practice started, one thing is certain—God forbids contacting any spirit unless it's the *Holy Spirit!*

Symbols of Halloween
Trick or Treat. Here are three of the possible origins of present day "trick or treating":

a. In the early practice of Halloween, people were afraid of spirits doing harm to their home, so they would leave treats outside their homes to keep them happy.
b. The Europeans tried to "Christianize" this pagan ritual by calling it "souling." They would go out and collect soul cakes. The more cakes you would receive, the more

prayers you would send up for your dead relatives.

c. In celebration of the recently completed harvest, Celts would give offerings of food to the gods. They often went from door to door to collect food to donate to their deities. History tells us that on Halloween the Celts would terrorize the countryside and populace, butcher cattle, and take it as spoil to please their gods.

Today's trick-or-treating consists of going from house to house and receiving candy from all the neighbors. Even if Halloween were totally harmless and free from pagan tradition, I would still be concerned about taking my children door-to-door and taking candy from people that I may not know. Throughout the rest of the year, we teach our children not to take anything from a stranger. But on Halloween we break our own rules!!!

The Jack o'Lantern. The Celts that lived in what is now Great Britain and northern France would carry a lantern when they walked on the eve of October 31. These lanterns were carved out of big turnips and the lights were believed to keep the evil spirits away. Children carved faces in the turnips, calling them "Jack o'lanterns." People later started to use the pumpkin in order to carry a bigger light.

The myth behind the Jack o'lantern was that a man named Jack made a pact with the devil and had to wander aimlessly through the darkness with only a piece of coal from hell in a turnip to guide him.

There are many people who believe that a person can never become a Christian because they have made a pact with the devil. This is not true. Before a person accepts Christ they *already* belong to the devil. In John 8:44a Jesus tell us, "You are of your father the devil, and the lusts of your father ye will do."

But inviting Jesus into their hearts *sets men free!* So, why would the devil make a deal with someone when they are already his? If you call on God to forgive you—no matter what your past was like—He will hear you today.

Witches. When we were growing up, we were always told that witches were make-believe. But, witches are real. The Bible talks about them in several passages. Today witchcraft is a very popular religion among our youth in America. Who would have ever thought that a seventeen-year-old honor student in Detroit, Michigan, could sue her school for the right to wear her pentagram, which is a symbol of her Wiccan religion. This is exactly what Crystal Seifferly did, according to the *Chicago Tribune*, February 10, 1999.

The Wiccan religion does not believe in the devil or Satan. They believe in five elementals, which are the false gods of forces. The five elementals are earth, wind, fire, water, and spirits. Witches do not claim to be devil worshippers. Witches do not believe the Bible is true so they will not accept a character from the Bible to worship. Many witches will hide behind environmentalism as a cover-up for the worship of Gaia, the goddess called "Mother Earth."

The Black Cat. The black cat has long been associated with witchcraft. Many superstitions have evolved about cats. It was believed that witches could change into cats. Some people also believed that cats were the spirits of the dead. Friends and relatives who had died would often return, with their souls inhabiting an animal—often a black cat. Black cats have remained a symbol of Halloween to the present. On the eve before their New Year (October 31), it was believed that Samhain called together all of the deceased. The dead would take different forms, with the evil spirits taking the form of animals—the most wicked taking the form of cats.

The belief in people coming back from the dead is *not* a Christian belief. That belief is called reincarnation. The Bible teaches that man dies only once. "And as it is appointed unto men once to die, but after this the judgment" (Hebrews 9:27).

Dressing in Costumes. During the festival of Samhain, there was a fire festival to honor the god of death. Sacred bonfires were lit on the tops of hills in honor of the false gods. History tells us that after the bonfire to Samhain, people were afraid to walk home in the dark. They were in fear of being possessed by spirits. So they dressed up in costumes and carved scary faces in their fire holders. They hoped that the spirits would be frightened and not bother them.

Without even knowing it, children in our society today continue this pagan practice by dressing up in various costumes. Pumpkins are now the objects of choice to carve faces into. The wearing of death masks is still used around the world in demon worship.

Three Things In Conclusion . . .

Abstain

In Deuteronomy 18:10–12, God gave His people **nine** things they were to stay away from. Many of the practices go hand in hand with the traditions of Halloween and go directly **against** God's Word.

1. **Human sacrifice**: In ancient times, they would offer children to false gods of fire. The bonfire was used by pagans who worshiped fire gods, like Baal. To appease these gods, they would offer children in the fire.
2. **Divination/fortune telling**: If you watch much TV, you can't miss the advertisements of psychics and people who are suppose to know your future. This practice is condemned in the Bible.
3. **Observer of times**: This is astrology. Christians do not believe that the stars can guide their life. Christians believe that God will guide our lives through His Word.
4. **Enchanter**: A person who uses chants to cast spells.
5. **Witch**: Witches are not make-believe characters. Exodus

22:18 says: "Thou shalt not suffer a witch to live." Though
New Testament Christians certainly do not condone the
Old Testament practice of executing witches, the fact is
they have become accepted, even heralded, members in
our culture today.

6. **Charmer**: Objects that are made by someone to protect
you or curse others.

7. **Consulter of familiar spirits**: A familiar spirit is a spirit
that impersonates a person who is dead.

8. **A wizard, magician, or sorcerer**: A person who uses magic to control people or uses occult practices to entice people into witchcraft.

9. **Necromancer**: Someone who claims to contact the dead.

Deuteronomy. 18:10–12 says:

> There shalt not be found among you any one that maketh
> his son or daughter to pass through the fire, or that useth
> divination, or an observer of times, or an enchanter, or a
> witch, or a charmer, or a consulter with familiar spirits, or
> a wizard, or a necromancer. For all that do these things are
> an abomination unto the LORD: and because of these abom-
> inations the Lord thy God doth drive them out from before
> thee.

You may have another question: What should I do with those
things in my life that are associated with witchcraft? Follow
Acts 19:18-19 which states:

> And many that believed came, and confessed, and shewed
> their deeds. Many of them also which used curious arts
> brought their books together, and burned them before all
> men: and they counted the price of them, and found it fifty
> thousand pieces of silver.

So, what is the answer to our opening question—should a Christian be involved with the pagan holiday of Halloween? No! Ephesians 5:11 says, "And have no fellowship with the unfruitful works of darkness, but rather reprove them." Not only should a Christian not partake in evil, *we are to expose it!*

Refocus

If there is any single thing Christians need to do on October 31, it is to pray! This is the highest unholy day of those in the occult. Witches believe that the separation between the natural and spiritual worlds is thinnest during this day. So, if for no other reason, the amount of evil supernatural activity is going to be greatest that day just because more occultism is being practiced. Also, it is known that more sacrifice (animal and yes, human) is carried out on October 31 than on all of the other days of the year combined. Christians—full of the Holy Ghost and fire—should be praying and conducting spiritual warfare against the powers of darkness! Along with Christ-centered celebrations of life and activities for our kids, churches should consider some teaching from the above information we've shared followed by a power-packed time of prayer, binding the forces of darkness and asking God to protect our neighborhoods, cities and citizens.

But there is a more important question . . .

Submit

Christ is asking for our obedience, but first He wants our hearts. He is willing that **anyone** who calls on His name can be saved and be delivered from darkness. Witch, Satanist, murderer . . . it doesn't matter, He can and will forgive you! Praise God!

The steps to salvation are simple.

▪ You must admit that you have sinned against God. **"For all** have sinned, and come short of the glory of God" (Romans 3:23).

- You must understand the penalty for sin is death. **"For the wages of sin is death; but the gift of God is eternal life through Jesus Christ our Lord"** (Romans 6:23).
- You need to understand that God loves you no matter what you have done. **"But God commendeth his love toward us, in that, while we were yet sinners, Christ died for us"** (Romans 5:8)
- You must confess that Jesus Christ is the true Messiah and receive His gift of salvation. **"That if thou shalt confess with thy mouth the Lord Jesus, and shalt believe in thine heart that God hath raised him from the dead, thou shalt be saved. For with the heart man believeth unto righteousness; and with the mouth confession is made unto salvation"** (Romans 10: 9–10).

Chapter 18
What Then Must We Do?

No Victory Without a Price

Be not ye therefore partakers with them. For ye were sometimes darkness, but now are ye light in the Lord: walk as
children of light: (For the fruit of the Spirit is in all good-
ness and righteousness and truth;) Proving what is acceptable unto the Lord. And have no fellowship with the unfruitful works of darkness, but rather reprove [expose] them.
—Ephesians 5:7–11

So now, we come to the menacing question, *"How bad do you
really want victory?"*

As you have read this book, you have seen how these authors take great concern for how the church is adversely affected by the elements of the world, the occult in particular.
Being separated from the world is a scary thought for many
believers. We want it both ways. But again, this spells disas-
ter sooner or later. So many of us want the benefits of Christianity but not the commitment. Our casual acceptance of
the philosophies all around us can short-circuit nearly every
part of our Christian walk and can certainly derail our ability to stave off spiritual attacks. By aligning ourselves with

the world system, in particular its entertainment, we are guaranteed to stifle the work of the Holy Spirit in our lives. Many would brush off this suggestion by saying, "It's only entertainment. I know it's only acting or make-believe. How can that be so wrong? How can it hurt me? After all, I *AM* a Christian . . . I can handle it!" It is to those of you still not convinced of our concern to whom we want to speak directly. We can't live your life for you, but we pray you'll consider what we're about to say, for we care about you earnestly.

The Faces of Sin

By giving ungodly entertainment our time, mind, money, emotions—even though we ourselves are not involved physically, it is the *same* as if we were actually participating. In Romans 1:29–31 Paul lists many of the sinful practices of the world. Then in verse thirty-two he states this:

> Who knowing the judgment of God, that they which commit such things are worthy of death, not only do the same, but have pleasure in them that do them.

He is saying that those who take pleasure in such sins are the same as those actually *committing* the sins!

We want to quote the study notes from Romans 1:32 found in the *Full Life Study Bible* published by Zondervan. It states:

> This disposition is the ultimate in depravity—vicarious enjoyment of lust and evil. Sin becomes entertainment. . . . Being entertained by watching other people sin and engage in ungodly actions, even while you yourself abstain, brings you under the same divine condemnation as those engaging in such evil practices. . . . Those (and especially those who profess faith in Christ) who use the immoral actions of others for entertainment and enjoyment are (also)

directly contributing to public opinion favorable to immorality and therefore to the corruption and eternal damnation of an indefinite number of other people. This sin is worthy of death and will be exposed and judged at the final day of judgment (2 Thessalonians 2:12).

To put it simply, if you are watching pornography, for example, you are under the same judgment as if you were actually committing the acts of sin!

Separation from the world's system is not intended by God to constrict us, but rather to free us. God intends for us to enjoy the benefits of separation. This is why His Word so clearly condemns fellowship with the world. We just can't have it both ways. Read here in 2 Corinthians 6:14–18 as He both warns us and also offers His rich rewards for obedience.

> Be ye not unequally yoked together with unbelievers: for what fellowship hath righteousness with unrighteousness? and what communion hath light with darkness? And what concord hath Christ with Belial? or what part hath he that believeth with an infidel? And what agreement hath the temple of God with idols? for ye are the temple of the living God; as God hath said, I will dwell in them, and walk in them; and I will be their God, and they shall be my people. Wherefore come out from among them, and be ye separate, saith the Lord, and touch not the unclean thing; and I will receive you, And will be a Father unto you, and ye shall be my sons and daughters, saith the Lord Almighty.

In the next verse (2 Corinthians 7:1) he exhorts us to accept God's plan.

> Having therefore these promises, dearly beloved, let us

cleanse ourselves from all filthiness of the flesh and spirit, perfecting holiness in the fear of God.

King David makes a very powerful and potent statement in Psalm 101:2–4.

> I will behave myself wisely in a perfect way. O when wilt thou come unto me? I will walk within my house with a perfect heart. I will set no wicked thing before mine eyes: I hate the work of them that turn aside; *it* shall not cleave to me. A froward heart shall depart from me: I will not know a wicked person.

He is saying that no vile thing shall enter his viewing and that he will not be partners with anyone who adheres to such things. Wow!

Disobedience Spells Certain Defeat!

Under Joshua's leadership, Israel knew nothing but victory against their enemies *until* the greed, lustful eyes, and particularly the disobedience of one man brought them defeat. In Joshua chapter seven we read of the defeat of Israel at Ai, causing the deaths of many, all because the man Achan had hidden items under his tent that God had proclaimed "off limits" for His people to possess. In this passage, the Hebrew word *cherem* is translated "accursed" in the King James Version, which is any object set apart for total extermination or annihilation. God had declared that everything Israel's enemies possessed should be destroyed. Nothing was to be taken as spoil, nor left untouched. The reason for this was that God was using Israel to carry out His judgment on the completely depraved tribes who inhabited the land. God wanted no remembrance of them to remain. *Cherem* could also be defined as items irrevocably consecrated for the use of idolatry or the demonic. But Achan had coveted and secretly possessed a Babylonian robe, some silver, and a bar of gold during Israel's taking of Jericho. It was for his secret sin that Achan and his family paid the ultimate price—death by stoning.

Just as with Israel and Achan, Saul and Israel lost God's protection and blessing in 1 Samuel 15 when he did not completely destroy the Amalekites and their possessions. Translate these stories into New Testament understanding and one can see that entire households are weakened and can lose their spiritual battles because of the actions, attitudes, and even physical possessions and practices of one member.

Even the world is now recognizing the physical effects of the wrong entertainment on the culture.

Eric recalls an edition of the NBC news magazine program, "The Brokaw Report," from 1992 when Tom Brokaw used a half hour of prime time TV to build a case which said that the number one reason we have teenage crime and related problems was due to the overwhelming adverse effects of rock music videos and slasher films! We find that pretty incredible that the seat of power for the liberal news media would be repeating the very same things we have found true for over fifteen years.

In Acts 19:18–20 it states that the Ephesian church, upon hearing Paul's preaching, brought together all items used for the glorification of demon gods and burned them. So what are we to do—burn all our CDs and tapes, smash our TVs, and live as hermits hoping for an immediate Rapture? Not necessarily, especially not the hermit part. Who then will tell the lost about the Savior? The items we may extract from our lives and rid our homes of depend on the content of the tapes or CDs and also on our ability to be self-controlled with the channel selector. If we can't control ourselves, then perhaps we need to put the TV in the garage for a season (and perhaps permanently in some cases). While we don't necessarily advocate large bonfires in your yard—or public displays which the world will not understand, we do believe that many in the church probably have bondages in their homes that need to be discarded.

What We Need Is a "God Attitude"!

Remember that once you come to Christ you are under the responsibility to see to it that nothing overtakes you and destroys your pure devotion to Him. Being addicted to anything can open the door and give Satan a foothold. If anything controls you, causes you to stumble, or becomes your master—even innocent things—run from it! Some things are just forbidden for us biblically. Other things may cause one of us to falter, but not another. It is certain that though we may be tempted to paint everything we personally see as wrong with the same brush, we each need to search the Word of God and search our hearts, following the leading of the Holy Spirit as He directs *our* individuals lives. It is certain also that if we attempt to walk the perilous tightrope between the world and the cross, we'll eventually become spiritually schizophrenic and fall toward the world. That's our fallen human nature which is always just lurking to drag us down.

Our thoughts and actions need to be focused on things above, and not on things that are below. God's Word is explicitly clear that instead of offering our time, affection, and financial resources to being entertained with the likes of violence, sexual promiscuity, sorcery, and demonism, we should offer ourselves wholly to Him. Through even just the sheer time we spend, don't we enter into a type of partnership with what entertains us? Of course. We are deceiving ourselves if we think we actually remain neutral to the content while being entertained by stories and scripts inundated with evil. When we allow images and sounds that we *know* are wrong into our lives, we are open game for Satan in Spiritual Warfare. Who cares if everybody else is doing it? We need to instill values and character that will help our kids swim against the stream of peer pressure that they will be facing all of their earthly lives. If they find it irresistible to turn down the latest entertainment fads today, will it be likewise when someone offers them a joint tomorrow? If not, they will surely be pushovers for Antichrist in the days ahead.

The Trap of Legalism

We have talked a great deal about things to watch out for and avoid. But now we want to address the tendency some may have to overreact. Some who read this might already be in or be tempted to fall into asceticism. It can be as deadly as the attitude that proclaims, "If it feels good, do it." Asceticism is the belief that one could attain a higher intellectual or spiritual plain through abstaining from various activities. In this case, it is the idea that if we just don't watch the wrong shows or do the wrong things that somehow God will then love us more. It is impossible to somehow (by our works no less) convince God to love or accept you anymore than He already does. How can the embodiment of love, love anymore completely? It's as if people think there is a brownie point system, allowing us a more intimate walk with the Lord for shunning things. It can easily become legalism. Once we are saved, we cannot get "more saved" by all that we avoid. And while it is true that the Bible is replete with the command "thou shalt not," it is repeated from cover to cover for our own good, not to spoil our pleasure or to constrict or bind us. Quite the opposite is true. Plus, to live an austere life, which concentrates on abstinence, can lead to pride ("Well, at least I don't attend movies or watch *that* show . . ." etc).

It isn't what we don't do that makes us holy. Holiness is not defined altogether by what we abstain from. Staying away from the wrong influences is simply called *obedience*! Holiness is defined by our heart attitude toward Jesus and our desire to follow Him. Jesus Himself made this clear when He said, "If ye love me, keep my commandments." Some of us need to concentrate more on all the stuff God instructed us to do, and less on what He told us not to do. Kingdom business should be our agenda. If we'd do that, there wouldn't be enough time or energy left to do the wrong stuff!

YOU Are a Priest of God!

And they shall teach my people the difference between the holy and profane, and cause them to discern between the unclean and the clean.

—Ezekiel 44:23

In the Old Testament it was the responsibility of the priests to make clear the difference between what was good and pure before the Lord and that which was evil. In our covenant with God, it is now the responsibility of the Christian. The New Testament clearly points to us as magistrates of God in a royal priesthood.

Hebrews 5:14 continues this saying:

But strong meat belongeth to them that are of full age, even those who by reason of use have their senses exercised to discern both good and evil.

This passage is telling us to continually use the solid meat or strong food of the Word of God to teach ourselves the difference between right and wrong. This is a heritage we need so desperately to pass along to our children and their children. It is part of our responsibility and privilege as priests for the Lord within our families.

We have the awesome responsibility to channel and direct our kids toward Christ. Both parents, children, and these authors—everyone—also has the responsibility to follow the sound directive of Philippians 4:8 which says:

> Finally, brethren, whatsoever things are true, whatsoever things are honest, whatsoever things are just, whatsoever things are pure, whatsoever things are lovely, whatsoever things are of good report; if there be any virtue, and if there be any praise, think on these things.

Perhaps this passage should be on a sign placed above our television sets, but more so, it should be engraved on our hearts. We need to also examine the sheer time many of us seem to spend on worldly entertainment. When you consider this, is it any wonder that many of our young people are so biblically illiterate? Again, the amount of time spent on being entertained as opposed to the Bible, prayer, Christian service, and fellowship speaks volumes. How we spend our free time, where we are making volitional choices, usually reveals who our "god" really is. Time spent with the wrong friends, entertainment, and influences will slowly erode even the strongest Christian life.

One great way to initially break the hold that TV, movies, and the wrong entertainment may have is to begin to pray for the entertainers, writers, producers, etc. For example, when we start praying for a rock star to be saved, it won't be long before we aren't as interested in his music as we are his soul. From personal experience, we have seen it work time and again.

Staying Connected

> Beware lest any man spoil you through philosophy and vain deceit, after the tradition of men, after the rudiments of the world, and not after Christ.
>
> —Colossians 2:8

This book has dealt a great deal with spiritual things, the workings of the enemy, and our authority as believers. But we need to address something that could enhance the spiritual victory level of your home that has nothing directly to do with what we've discussed in these pages.

As parents, if there is any single piece of advice we want to impart to you, it is STAY CONNECTED. It is a fact that many teens try very hard to disconnect from their parents. There is a time to "let go," but it must be the *right* time. Until it is that right time for you, here is some advice from our hearts to help you stay the course and win the fight against the Evil One.

The moment we as parents let down our care, concern, and inquisitiveness about our kids and their lives, the world and its value system is right there to fill up the void. Besides love and acceptance, kids today are longing for parents who care what they are all about. Though they may not always acknowledge it and may in fact rebel against it, deep down inside, kids and teens want to know where the limits are, where the lines are drawn, and who is in charge.

Our society continues to prod, even shout at us to do our "own thing." We see children falling into the trap of defying authority at alarmingly early ages now and with horrific results. Watch the news, listen to the talk shows, and read the accounts. It is everywhere. Kids, without a value system, floating aimlessly without a rudder in a sea of upheaval, searching for the elusive thing that only parents can give them. That sometimes intangible but most important element—moral guidelines, accompanied by consequences. This instills purpose for life itself and is the single thing kids are *really* craving. "Let me be me!" they may insist, but underneath the adolescent assertiveness they are really screaming, "Show me the way!"

We both learned the hard way and it cost us dearly. We

were a couple of Satan's best workers and he used us every chance he got, which was often. The progression the culture has taken is to a large part due to the widening disconnect between parents and their offspring. Who do you suppose is working full blast to enlarge that chasm? Of course, Lucifer is and any of us could be his next victim—if we let down our guard.

You are NOT doing your kids a service by "giving them space." That is a cop-out. Please understand we are not commending the overbearing parent who rules with an iron fist. What we are saying is that it is our responsibility to first plant and water the seeds that teach, instruct, and correct our children. Then, we must continue following up on what else it is that they are learning. For example, if you don't know who your fifteen-year-old is keeping for friends, you had better find out, and now! Friends are fast becoming what hopefully you have always been—the role model. The idea that a parent doesn't want to encroach upon their kids and thus allows them to do what they fancy, unbridled and unsupervised, is perhaps the supreme disservice being done to our youth today.

Eric is reminded of a night back around 1990 when he came face to face with a mother who had believed she was loving her son by allowing him his friends, his time, and his activities, all without any parental guidance or supervision.

One evening, as I was ministering in a local church, I encountered the ultimate price that Satan extracts from a disconnected parent. At the close of my seminar, I extended the invitation for anyone who needed salvation or to spend time with the Lord to come forward. As people filed forward, a group of ladies came to the altar literally holding up one woman. She was weeping uncontrollably and could barely walk. I remember coming down from the platform and whispering to one of the attending ladies, "What is happening with her?" I was told that the son of the disturbed woman had committed suicide just a few days prior. I will never forget how I felt as the details were recounted to me.

This young mother had decided to give her son unobstructed freedom. In doing so, she thought that it would bond them somehow and that he would like and appreciate it. When the police investigated his death, it came to light that his mother had not entered her son's room in over **TWO YEARS**! Upon returning home one evening, she had occasion to call for her son and when he did not answer after repeated attempts, she opened the door to find him dead of a self-inflicted shotgun wound. When she opened the door, she found something else besides her son. She found a room dedicated to satanic worship. Her son had painted the room completely black. Mixed in with the collection of the heaviest of heavy metal albums and tapes were the candles and ceremonial knives used in satanic rituals. Numerous occult books laid about. And on the floor was painted a large five-pointed star, the pentagram. This mother had no idea that any of this was right under her roof because she was totally disconnected from her son's life—thinking all the while that it was okay. **IT IS NOT OKAY!**

The price paid by this mother is very similar to the one paid by a man named Eli in the Old Testament. The exception was that Eli *knew* his sons were offering "strange fire" before the altar of God, yet he did nothing to try and stop them. The best he could muster was the question, "Why do you do such things?" which was hardly an effort. His slack attitude ended in the tragic death of both of his sons.

We are not inferring that this is a common occurrence,

for gratefully, it is not. Nor are we telling you that neglect will actually drive your son or daughter into Satan's arms. But it opens the door for demonic tentacles to begin intertwining themselves slowly but strongly into the fabric of your child or teen's life. Thankfully, not all families who let their kids go unchecked end up in a story as tragic as this one, but will you take the chance on allowing your disconnect with your kids to undo not only your dream for them, but God's desire as well? The Lord has entrusted them to you for these short years to mold, mentor, love, and cherish. If there is any single thing that will *disarm the powers of darkness* in our homes today it is staying connected to your kids.

As we discussed instances from our ministry travels, David brought up a personal experience that really speaks about the root cause of many of our youth's dilemmas.

A lady approached me one evening in a church and asked me to speak to her daughter. She said, "My daughter is messed up and needs help." I asked her if they attended church and she said no. I asked her if she (the mother) was a Christian and she said no and then repeated to me that it was her daughter that needed help, not her. I told her that we needed to take care of her spiritual problems first. Becoming irritated, she insisted that she was fine but her daughter was messed up. I repeated that we needed to settle her spiritual future first, but to no avail. She finally become incensed and walked away.

You see, this mother wanted David to "fix" the problems of her daughter, but didn't want to come to grips with her own need. Expecting a quick fix—by a total stranger—is often the desire of parents who have lost control but are not willing to examine the hopelessness of their own lives first. Chances are this mother wanted her daughter to stop acting a particular way, but without a change of *heart* and a cleansing of the soul, any changes David might have been able to talk the girl into making would have been only surface adjustments. It's kind of like getting the car tuned up when, in reality, your engine is ready to throw a piston rod. It might make you *think* things are okay because you did "something," but it won't be long before you are stranded on the roadside and going nowhere. The "band-aid" approach doesn't work on heart attack victims and it won't work on lives stained from years of sin. The only hope is for a trained doctor to open you up and do surgery.

People sometimes think that we in "the ministry" can just wave our hand and fix things. In reality, however, we in ourselves can do *nothing*. We just happen to work for the Specialist this mother and daughter from David's story needed to see. Any words David would have spoken would have had a benign effect unless the mother and daughter would have been willing to call in Dr. Jesus and allow Him to do His surgery. He's the only one who knows how to *really* fix the problems. And once He does, if we'll just cooperate in the "recovery," it's guaranteed to straighten things out, clean up the mess, and give us an everlasting "heart" with valves that pump a unique and powerful *blood*!

Though there are no guarantees in this life, children growing up in a home with loving parents, in a stable, biblical environment, anchored to a local Bible-believing church, have a better opportunity of avoiding some of the enormous pitfalls and traps of this world today. We know that this is a loaded statement because it doesn't always work out that way every time. We can't live our kid's lives for them and we can't make them live for the Lord. They are free agents and we are not God. Some kids get sideways with the Lord or have a bad experience with other Christians or fall into the wrong crowd or rebel or any of a thousand other things. But the picture we describe of a good home and church environment is certainly much better than the alternative, isn't it?

We also know that there are going to be strong Christians who are on fire for God who will read this who came from secular or even occult laden homes. Perhaps they just "happened" into the church one day. Maybe they came to Sunday school as a result of a bus ministry outreach. God only knows. But they saw their hopeless condition and need for Jesus and turned out making a powerful impact for heaven. How we thank God for His mercy!

Then there are the "nominal" church kids who come from a Christian home but without the benefit of strong, vital parental input and direction in their lives. They are the ones who cause trouble at youth camp or make fun during youth Bible study. Again, they are free moral agents, but if they come from a less than stellar Christian home—okay, let's say it, a rotten home where the parents only *claimed* to be Christians —then chances are these kids will end up being harder to convince about heaven, hell, the Bible, and their need for salvation than those who grew up with atheists. Our point is, one of the strongest elements of Spiritual Warfare that is bound to give the devil fits is when you sacrifice *time* for your family, which is really what this all boils down to.

Church membership and *the loving and strong mentoring of two parents* give children at least a fighting chance to avoid some of the cesspools life offers for them to be poisoned with. Both these authors are grateful for what the Lord has done, but we wonder if Eric would have been a promiscuous drug addict or if David would have ever seen the inside of a reform school had we experienced the kind of environment we've described as our ideal.

Both of us have had to be careful when speaking of these issues because the human reaction is often one of guilt. We are **NOT** trying to lay a guilt trip on anyone but instead to raise up the standard of holiness that is certain to glorify God and tear down Satan's kingdom.

Once, years ago, a man attending one of Eric's seminars on the entertainment world came rushing forward during the closing invitation and altar time. Having come to church straight from work and dressed in his oily clothes, this mechanic wept like a baby. He told Eric that he felt so guilty for letting his children watch "all that stuff," that he didn't know how he could ever forgive himself. Eric's immediate response was, "Brother, there is therefore now no condemnation to them which are in Christ Jesus!" That wonderful freeing passage from Romans 8:1 has been in Eric's seminar ever since.

True, you can't change yesterday. Satan wants you to be filled with regret and remorse in what you may have allowed in your home in the past. But all you can do is refuse to accept that accusation from the Deceiver, ask for God's forgiveness and help, and walk on. You don't get another chance at the past, but you do have a choice as to how you will live tomorrow. Make the most of it for Christ!

And Finally, Persevere!

Now therefore fear the LORD, and serve him in sincerity and in truth: and put away the gods which your fathers served on the other side of the flood, and in Egypt; and serve ye the LORD. And if it seem evil unto you to serve the LORD, choose you this day whom ye will serve; whether the gods which your fathers served that were on the other side of the flood, or the gods of the Amorites, in whose land ye dwell: but as for me and my house, we will serve the LORD.
—Joshua 24:14-15

Make the decision that nothing will stand in your way, that you will, by faith, walk through all circumstances, trials, and trouble, and that you and Jesus equal a majority! The key to winning in Spiritual Warfare, as well as victory in your home, boils down to first learning and then using the weapons and insight God gives us. But perhaps the most important tool beyond this is perseverance. Don't quit! Don't give up! In Christ, all victory is found!

- Dedicate yourself to prayer.
- Dedicate yourself to teach your family the elements of Spiritual Warfare.
- Be resolute that fear will have no place in you.
- Make the decision to be more than just hearers of the truth, but doers of the truth.
- Resolve that when you stand before the Lord you will have done everything to stand firm here on earth (Ephesians 6:13) and that the last few words of Joshua 24:15 will have been your battle cry—". . . but as for me and my house, we will serve the LORD!"

Chapter 19

Our Last Word

It would be tragic to write this book, exposing the devil's works and speaking of attaining the great victory that Christians have in Christ, and yet leave any reader with a question about the Lord's plan for salvation. There is NO winning in Spiritual Warfare without a personal relationship with Christ. It is paramount to every aspect.

Eternity is only a heartbeat away for all of us. Today, thousands of people around the world will enter eternity without Jesus Christ as Lord and Savior of their lives. The tragedy is that so many will never think about what an eternity without Jesus means. It is eternal death, suffering, loneliness, and pain. By not accepting God's tremendous offer of salvation, man is doomed. However, if you are still breathing, there is hope! Eternity with Jesus is peace, joy, rest, and love. It is a future that ALL Christians look forward to.

This eternal salvation is free to all, but does not come by merely claiming to be a Christian or by doing good works or observing the ordinances of the church such as membership, baptism, communion, or tithing. Christianity is not inherited either. No, it is an act of your personal will. The free gift of salvation can be obtained only through honest, heartfelt repentance.

Examine your life. Where would you be for all eternity if for you that last heartbeat happened today? Not sure? You can be.

Romans 10:9–10 tells us:

> That if thou shalt confess with thy mouth the Lord Jesus, and shalt believe in thine heart that God hath raised him from the dead, thou shalt be saved.

Not "might be" or "could be." You have God's promise on it. You *will be* saved.

Many people do not know how to pray, so here is a sample prayer to pray.

> Dear Lord Jesus, I know that I am a sinner and I believe you died on the cross for me. I believe that you were buried and rose again as the Scripture says. The best I know how, I want to ask you to forgive me of all my sins and save me. Fill me with your Holy Spirit that I may serve you all the days of my life. I pray this prayer in the name of my Lord and Savior, Jesus Christ. Amen.

If you have any doubts, stop right now and invite Jesus to come into your heart. Just simply ask Him to save you and then turn from sin and to the pages of the Bible instead. It will be the most important thing you will ever do.

—Eric Barger and David Benoit

Eric Barger (Bar-jer) is a well known conference speaker, author, and evangelist with a no-nonsense message for today. His challenging, biblically based "Take A Stand!" Seminar series has been held in churches across North America since 1984. Coming from the world of rock music as a professional musician, recording engineer, and record producer, Eric was lost in New Age mysticism and drug addiction. Then, in 1981, he met Jesus Christ! Eric is now a recognized author of several books including the Christian bestseller, *From Rock to Rock*. He has written for *USA Today* and has been featured on the Trinity Broadcasting Network, "Point of View with Marlin Maddoux," and "Truths That Transform" with Dr. D. James Kennedy, as well as in hundreds of other electronic and print media interviews. His evangelical teaching ministry concerning issues such as the New Age movement, the cults, spiritual warfare, and current events in the light of Bible prophecy is headquartered in the Dallas, Texas, area where he resides with his wife, Melanie. To bring him to your church, to receive his free newsletter, or to request a materials list, contact

Take A Stand! Ministries
P.O. Box 1485
Rowlett, TX 75030
or online at *www.ericbarger.com.*

David Benoit (Ben-wah) accepted Christ as Savior in 1972 after a rebellious teenage life had led him to reform school. He is now a graduate of Liberty Baptist College (now Liberty University). In 1984, he founded Glory Ministries, an evangelistic ministry. His expertise in exposing the New Age movement and the occult led him to author two books, *Fourteen Things Witches Hope Parents Never Find Out* and *Who's Watching the Playpen?* He has hosted his own daily radio talk show in Dallas, been interviewed on various Christian programs including the Inspirational Network, Trinity Broadcasting Network, Moody Broadcasting, "Point of View with Marlin Maddoux," Dr. D. James Kennedy, and Bob Larson Live. He is also a frequent guest host for the Southwest Radio Church program. David has the rare ability to communicate his message to young people, as well as to parents, using humor and interesting facts. His goal is to strengthen the family and to give them the biblical tools they need to live in these troubled times. David resides in Dallas, Texas, with his wife Debbie, and children, Brandon and Lindsay. Contact him through

Glory Ministries
P.O. Box 864317
Plano, TX 75086